What Martin's students say about him

'I got a copy of Martin's book to have a read through to help with my nerves and most of all my understanding of becoming a safe driver. I was a bag of nerves, but after reading this book everything was made to look so much easier and it helped me massively. I highly highly recommend this book.'

Carly – Thatcham

'Really good book, highly recommend! Explains everything you need to know clearly and is easy to understand!'

Estelle – Wantage

'I think Martin's book is perfect for any driver, even those that have passed their test. It is structured in a very logical and chronological order starting with the basics and moving through to more complex topics making it the perfect book for any driver at any level. The clear diagrams and explanations are also very useful in terms of enhancing understanding and slowly building knowledge. I recommend this book to anyone wishing to pass their test first time.'

Barnaby – Bradfield

'A really great book, from a driving instructor I would highly recommend. The book helps to outline manoeuvres and skills and enables you to carry one learning WITH EASE, even when your lesson has finished.'

Holly – Silchester

LEARN TO DRIVE...
an EASIER WAY

Simple advice to help you to become a
safe, competent and confident driver

Martin Caswell
DVSA ADI Grade A

with illustrations by David Turbitt and Clare Clarke

Published by
Filament Publishing Ltd
16, Croydon Road, Waddon, Croydon,
Surrey, CR0 4PA, United Kingdom
Telephone +44 (0)20 8688 2598
Fax +44 (0)20 7183 7186
info@filamentpublishing.com
www.filamentpublishing.com

ISBN 978-1-910819-67-8

Printed by IngramSpark

Second Edition 2020.

Contents

Acknowledgements

I'd like to start by thanking Nick James, who encouraged me to write this book and who introduced me to Chris Day, of Filament publishing. Chris, of course, deserves thanks for his never-ending encouragement and support, along with his production manager Zara Thatcher.

My gratitude also goes to book publicist Helen Lewis and designer Lisa Snape, for their help and support.

Thanks go to my editor, Charlotte Fleming, for all her hard and devoted work and to Dave Turbitt, whose illustrations have brought this book to life, as well as Clare Clarke for additional illustrations.

I would like to thank Alicia Caswell, my wife, for her support, encouragement and for putting up with being abandoned for long nights and into the early hours.

Perhaps most importantly, I would like to thank all my pupils that I have taught since August 19th 1974, and who have taught me how to teach and to simplify. They are the inspiration for this book and I could not have got here without them.

Thanks to all of those who bought the first edition of my book, Learners and many driving instructors, who are using my book as a 'Learning Tool'.

Martin Caswell

Introduction

'Learning to drive is rather like doing a jigsaw puzzle. No matter how smart you are, unless you have all the pieces, you will never make a complete picture.'

If you are reading this book, you are probably a new driver, or about to become one. The best way to learn to drive is to get out on the roads and learn by doing, but that doesn't mean you can't be prepared when you do.

Becoming a confident driver takes more than just learning mechanical skills. It is also having the right mindset behind the wheel, the ability to 'read' the road ahead and to anticipate trouble long before it arises. Understanding how the car works, how the road works and how your own head works is an important part of becoming a competent driver. The good news is: you already know most of that already, and this book can show you the rest.

I have been a driving instructor for over 40 years, which means I have spent more than 75,000 hours teaching Learner Drivers, conducting Intensive Courses, Refresher Driving Lessons, as well as Advanced Driving, Skid Control and Instructor training. In this time, I have learned a lot about driving and a lot about learning. Learning something new doesn't mean you have to start from nothing, there is already so much you know that can help you get to grips with driving.

For example, you've been a pedestrian a lot longer than you've been a driver: if you were to cross the road as a pedestrian, when would you step out? You would emerge when driving using exactly the same decision-making skills that you know about cars, road-safety and how quickly you can react in any situation. Where motorists get into difficulties is when they behave in a way when driving that they would never even consider behaving as a pedestrian.

Just like learning anything new, you take what you know already, you add some new information, and you practice. The Easier Way is to make the most of what you already know and understand. Not only does this mean you can concentrate on the elements that really are unique to driving, but you can start learning to drive with the confidence that most of what you need to do isn't new at all.

You can read this book from cover to cover, or you can use it as a reference book in partnership with your driving lessons. However you want to use it, this book will show you, through explanation, examples, diagrams and analogies, that there really is an easier way to learn to drive.

'Like learning to ride a bike for the first time – it seems daunting at first, but when you know how it's done, you can't imagine why you were so nervous to begin with.'

📄 A little note on safety:

When I first started teaching I had an elderly lady in her seventies who came to me for driving lessons. She came out with a great phrase which I have quoted to so many of my pupils over the years, which goes like this:

'It is better to be 30 minutes late in this world... than 30 years early in the next'

Now this is great, and so true. This is what will keep you safe. It is obviously much better to arrive late for something, than not arrive at all. Just remember this when someone you are waiting for is late, or when you are rushing to get somewhere.

This applies as much today, if not more so in this busy world we live in, as it did all those years ago.

When you are driving you need to be fully concentrating on the task in hand and not be distracted by anything else. The majority of accidents, major or minor, are caused by those who are distracted by something unrelated to driving. You need to be prepared for the unexpected at all times – the unexpected is most likely to happen when you are distracted and not ready to react.

Remember that you are driving a lethal weapon. Your vehicle has the potential to injure or kill other road users, your passengers or yourself.

Think about how it would feel to have injured or killed someone. No amount of regret can reverse that event. How will you feel when confronted by your victim's loved ones? How will you feel when being interrogated by a lawyer in a court of law? How important was that task which took your concentration away at that vital moment?

When driving, concentrate on driving. Any other tasks can, and should, only be done when you are parked up safely.

Keep Safe... and keep everyone else safe too!

KNOW THE ESSENTIALS

In the driving seat

Under the bonnet

Legal Obligations

Testing

In the driving seat

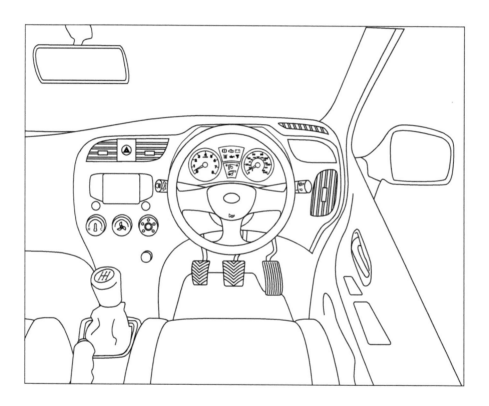

Pedals

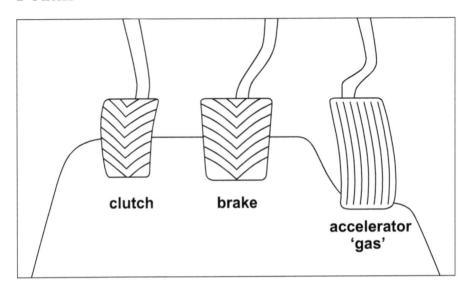

The pedal on the right is the **Accelerator** pedal and is operated with the right foot. Pressing this pedal will increase the car's speed, and lifting off this pedal will allow the car to slow down.

Commonly referred to as the 'gas' pedal by most driving instructors, you will normally be told to 'press the gas', 'less gas', 'off the gas' or 'set the gas'. The last one you will normally do when setting off from standstill.

The pedal in the middle is the **Brake** pedal and is also operated by the right foot. The brake pedal enables you to slow down or stop the car. Otherwise referred to as the footbrake (as distinct from the handbrake), the pedal operates all four wheels of the car and switches on the rear brake lights.

Brakes are useful for 3 things: slowing the vehicle, stopping the vehicle, and – very importantly – for giving you 'time'. Time to assess the situation around your vehicle, time to get gear changes completed, time to assess and re-assess the situation. Above all, the brake gives you time to bring your vehicle to a safe and controlled stop if necessary.

Normally you will be told to 'brake gently', 'brake to stop' or 'cover the brake'. When asked to 'cover' the brake, it doesn't mean to press it down necessarily, but just to find the brake so that you are ready if you need to use it. You will also notice that the brake pedal doesn't go all the way down to the floor like the gas and clutch pedal will, so when you first use the brake pedal for the very first time, treat it with respect: it doesn't take very much pressure to bring the car to stop. This pedal can be very sensitive on most modern cars and it may stop quicker than you were expecting.

The pedal on the far left is the **Clutch** pedal and is operated by the left foot. This is the only pedal that the left foot operates. The clutch enables you to select or change a gear. Visualise the clutch being pushed down as 'opening a door' for the gear lever to go through.

You will also use the clutch, along with the gas pedal, when moving off from a stationary position, and when pushing down the brake to stop the car.

Again you may be asked to 'clutch down', 'clutch up' or 'cover the clutch'. When asked to 'cover' the clutch, it doesn't mean to press it down, but just to find the clutch so that you are ready if you need to use it.

Handbrake

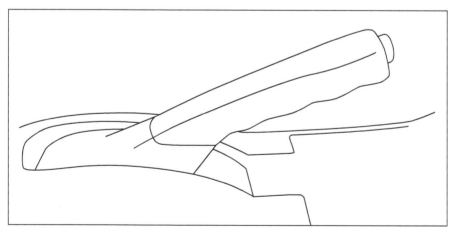

The handbrake, sometimes referred to as the parking brake, only operates the rear wheels of the car and doesn't switch on the rear brake lights. The handbrake just holds the car in the stopped position and prevents the car from rolling forward or back.

When the handbrake is 'on' the red handbrake warning light on the dash panel will also be showing. When you release the handbrake, the red warning light on the dash panel will go off. Do not try to drive if the red handbrake symbol is lit.

When you first get into the car, the handbrake should be already on and in the up position.

To release the handbrake, you will need to press the little button at the end of the lever, next to your thumb. Now, if you try to push this button you will find that it won't go in and the handbrake doesn't move. What you need to do is to pull the handbrake up a little at the same time as you press the button in. You can now release the handbrake by continuing to hold the button and allowing the handbrake to lower down as far as it will go – the warning light will go off. To put the handbrake on, press the button in and pull the handbrake up quite firmly until you feel some resistance and then release the button and the handbrake will stay in the up position and will hold the car still – the warning light will now go on.

Most importantly, when putting the handbrake on and pulling it up, remember to hold the button in. If you don't hold the button in you will hear a loud clicking noise: this is the ratchets on the handbrake being worn down. If you were to continue to do this over a period of time you would continue to wear those ratchets down until eventually the handbrake would no longer be capable of holding the car still.

> Remember, wherever you hear an unusal noise on the car it normally means additional wear and tear, or more fuel than is necessary is being used, adding more expense to your motoring costs.

Gear lever

The function of the gear lever, or gear stick, is to change from one gear to the next when you want to increase or reduce speed. To change gear, you need to push the clutch down fully to the floor and lift your right foot off the gas pedal.

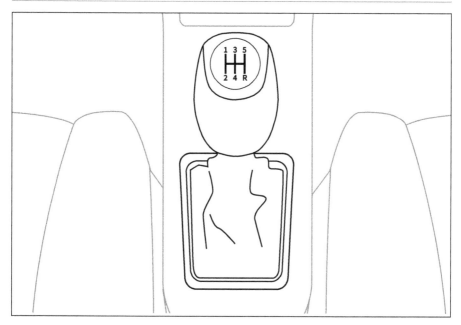

You may have heard the expression of changing 'up' a gear and changing 'down' a gear. Changing up a gear would be changing from first to second, second to third, third to fourth, fourth to fifth and, on some cars, fifth to sixth gear. Changing down a gear would be changing from sixth to fifth gear, fifth to fourth gear, and so on.

The gears are shown on the top of the gear lever, but you should avoid looking down at the gear lever, instead learn where each gear is positioned so that you can keep your eyes on the road at all times. The central position in the middle of the gear lever, between all of the gears, is called 'neutral'. When the gear lever is in this position it is not in any gear at all, and it should be possible to wobble the stick lightly from side to side.

The gear lever on modern cars – since the early 1960s – are spring-loaded. What this means is that when the gear lever is in the 'neutral' position, it centralises in the middle between third and fourth gear. If you push the gear lever to the far left towards first and second gear and then let it go, it will spring back to the middle position in line with third and fourth gear again. Likewise, if you pull the gear lever over towards fifth and sixth gear and then let it go, it will spring back to the central position between third and fourth gear.

To select any of the gears you should first of all push the clutch down with your left foot all the way to the floor. To select first gear push as far to the left as it will go and then push forward.

To change from first to second gear, keep pushing to the left and pull the gear lever straight back.

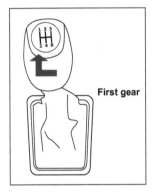 First gear

 Second gear

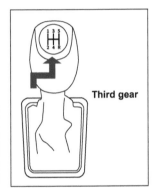 Third gear

To change from second to third gear, allow the spring to do the work. Very gently nudge the gear lever forward towards the neutral position, it will jump slightly to the right, so you can continue to push it gently forward into third gear.

To change from third gear to fourth gear – this is the easy one – just pull the gear lever straight back into fourth gear.

> To make it easier for you, aim the gears towards the four wheels of the car. First gear towards the front passenger side wheel, second gear towards the back passenger side wheel, third gear towards the front drivers side wheel and fourth gear towards the back drivers side wheel.

To change from fourth gear to fifth gear you are going to need to fight the spring a little by applying pressure to the right (pulling towards you) whilst it is still in fourth gear and keeping this

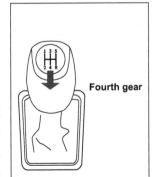 Fourth gear

 Fifth gear

pressure as you push forward. It will jump across to the right and you can pull it into fifth gear.

Reverse gear is shown on the top of the gear stick, and can be different in each car, so make sure to check which direction is reverse gear before you start driving. Don't worry too much about selecting this by mistake – most cars have a device to prevent you from selecting reverse without meaning to, most common is a little lever on the neck of the gear stick which you pull up before selecting reverse gear, in others, you may need to push the gear lever down. Your instructor will advise you for the car you are about to drive.

> If you're learning on a manual car, the driver sitting beside you must have a manual licence. If they have an automatic licence and you're driving a manual car, they are not legally entitled to sit with you, and you are driving illegally.

Steering wheel

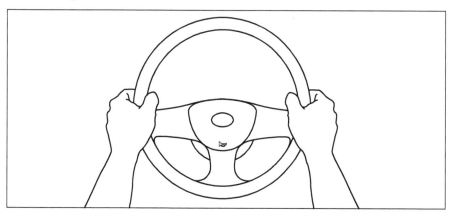

In the centre of the steering wheel is the airbag, which will respond to pressure to activate and help to prevent or lessen injuries in the event of a serious accident. Also you have a 'horn' icon. This is where you operate the horn of your car to warn another road user of your presence.

Imagine the steering wheel is the face of a clock. When driving along, the ideal position for your hands on the steering wheel would be at either the 'quarter to three' or 'ten to two' position, but in any case above the steering wheel spokes. If your hands are too low on the steering wheel it can restrict how much you are able to turn the steering wheel in the event of an emergency.

You should mentally divide the wheel into the 12 o'clock and 6 o'clock position. The left hand should avoid going to the right past the 12 o'clock and 6 o'clock position and the right hand should avoid going to the left past the 12 o'clock and 6 o'clock position as this will limit the amount you can turn the steering wheel, and could cause you to end up going wider than you planned.

When turning the steering wheel, you should feed it through your hands and not cross your hands without letting it slide through them. By crossing your hands one hand will be lifting completely off the steering wheel, thus compromising control, particularly if the one hand that is on the wheel should slip off. By feeding the wheel through your hands at all times you will have two hands on the steering wheel.

If you are you finding it difficult to turn the steering wheel without crossing your hands, practise when you get home with a large circular tray or large dinner plate. Practise turning it in a full circle to the right two or three times by keeping your left hand on the left-hand side and the right-hand on the right hand side of the plate, so that the left hand never crosses to the right-hand side and the right hand never crosses to the left-hand side. Once you've mastered turning a wheel to the right using this method, then start turning it to the left applying the same rules. Literally TWO minutes of practise is probably all that you will need. That's not two minutes every day, but just one two-minute session and you will find that it will just click and that you will have mastered how to steer safely.

Steering wheel stalks

INDICATOR ARM

When you want to change your road position or turn to the left or to the right, you will need to use your indicators to signal to other road users your intention.

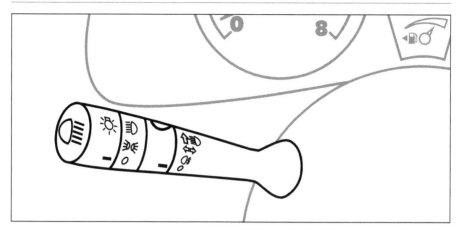

The indicator arm is normally on the left-hand side of the steering wheel. To signal your intention to turn to the right you will need to push the indicator arm upwards. To signal your intention to turn to the left, you will need to push the indicator arm downwards.

Whichever way you intend to turn the steering wheel, the indicator arm follows the direction of the steering wheel. So when you want to turn to the right, the left-hand side of the steering wheel will move up, and so does the indicator arm. When you want to turn to the left, the left-hand side of the steering wheel will move down, so does the indicator arm, so you push the indicator arm downwards.

When pushing the indicator arm upwards or downwards, be sure to keep both hands on the steering wheel and keep your left thumb hooked around the steering wheel rim, reaching out with just your fingers to operate the indicator arm. This way you will not compromise your steering and won't put too much pressure on the indicator arm itself.

In the old days, the indicator switch would be in the centre of the dash panel and you would flick the switch to the left or to the right, but of course you would only have one hand on the steering wheel while you were carrying out this action. So designers decided that it would be safer to move the indicator switch to the steering wheel so that you would keep both hands on the wheel while driving. If you take your hand off the steering wheel to operate the indicator arm, you have just defeated the idea of redesigning the car and improving steering safely.

This is also why the headlight switch on, most cars are situated on the indicator arm. When the headlights are on you can either have them on 'full beam' to see more of the road around you, or 'dipped' for when passing other cars and you don't want to dazzle the other drivers. To dip or raise the headlights normally requires you to just flick the indicator arm towards or away from you. Ask your instructor to show you how to do this on the car you are learning on, and the car you intend to drive.

WINDSCREEN WIPER ARM

Before you start off on a journey, particularly if it is raining or likely to start raining, you should familiarise yourself with the front and rear windscreen wiper and washer controls while you're still parked. This will ensure that it will be less of a distraction when you need to operate your windscreen wipers whilst you are driving along. Likewise, if it is likely to rain, be overcast, foggy or dark you should also familiarise with your headlight and fog-light switches too.

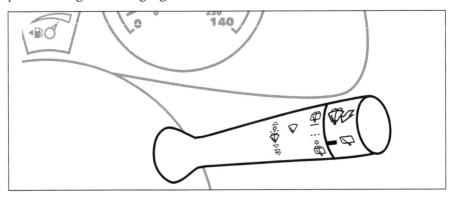

In most cars when the windscreen wiper arm is in the uppermost position the windscreen wipers are switched off. When pulled down one position, the wipers will operate intermittently and can sometimes be set to wiping once every 10 seconds, 5 seconds, 2 seconds etc. Pull down once more and the wipers will be on continuously, and the finally pull down again to put the wipers onto fast speed for heavy rain conditions.

The rear window wiper will often be operated by rotating the end of the windscreen wiper arm away from you by one click. This will generally put the rear windscreen wiper into the intermittent mode of once every 10 seconds. Rotate it once more and the rear wiper will be on continuously. When driving on quieter roads, the rear wiper can be set to intermittent, but on faster main roads, dual-carriageways or motorways, the water will be coming off the rear wheels onto the rear window much more rapidly, so switching to continuous would be necessary.

To clean the front windscreen and operate the windscreen washer, you will need to pull the windscreen wiper arm towards you and hold it for a couple of seconds. This will squirt water onto the windscreen and cause the windscreen wiper to go across the windscreen two or three times to clear the water off the screen.

To clean the rear window, you will normally rotate the end of the windscreen wiper arm towards you and hold it in that position for a few seconds. This will now squirt water on to the rear window and the windscreen wiper will go across two or three times to clear the water.

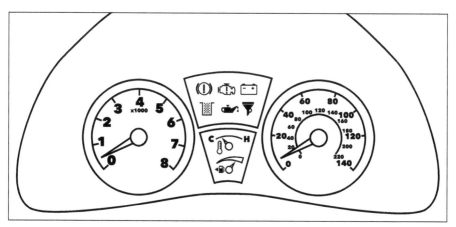

Dash Panel

The dials and lights on the dashboard of your car are there so you can be aware of how the car is functioning and adapt to ensure you are always driving safely. As a rule, there shouldn't be any red or orange warning lights showing. If any of these lights are on while driving, you will need to stop and investigate, or call or stop at a garage to minimise any damage to your car.

There are four important dials on the dashboard of any car: speedometer, rev counter, fuel gauge and temperature gauge.

SPEEDOMETER

On the speedometer, you will notice two sets of numbers: larger numbers on the outer area and smaller numbers on the inner area. The larger numbers are miles per hour, the smaller numbers are kilometres. If you were to drive your car in Europe the speeds are set in kilometres. If you see a sign stating 100, it doesn't mean 100 miles per hour, but 100 kilometres per hour. As you will see on the dial, 100 kilometres is the equivalent of 62 miles per hour – it means that you don't have to do the mathematics while driving. Generally we are only really interested in the miles per hour or mph.

REV COUNTER

Here you have the 'rev counter'. As you press the accelerator or 'gas' pedal, the needle will move up and as you lift your foot off the accelerator the needle will drop down. This shows you how much power you're setting to take up the load or weight of the car as you move off and as you're driving along.

FUEL GAUGE

You will also notice that there is a fuel gauge to let you know how much fuel you currently have. It is always a good idea to make sure that you have plenty of fuel before you set off on any journey. If you allow the fuel to get too low, a little orange fuel pump will be displayed on the dashboard warning you that you only have a few miles in which to find a petrol station. A word of warning, don't drive too long with the fuel light on, as you may run out of fuel entirely, and find yourself stranded.

TEMPERATURE GAUGE

Just like you if you were to go for a walk or run, the engine will get warmer as it is driven. And also just like you, it isn't healthy for the engine to get too hot or too cold.

Most modern cars no longer have a temperature gauge, but some still do. The cars without a temperature gauge will normally show a blue 'thermometer' icon when started up from cold and as the engine warms up this blue will go out. If the engine begins to seriously overheat the thermometer icon will come on, showing red. If this is the case then you should begin to look for a safe and convenient place to stop as soon as you can, in order to minimise any damage to your car engine.

For those cars that have an actual temperature gauge when the engine is started up from cold, the needle will be pointing to the blue side of the gauge. As the engine warms up the temperature gauge needle will normally settle around a quarter to half way across the gauge. But if the temperature gauge needle should start to get very close to the red area, then again you should begin to look for a safe and convenient place to stop as soon as you can and let your engine cool, to minimise any damage to your car engine.

Mirrors

CENTRE INTERIOR REAR-VIEW MIRROR

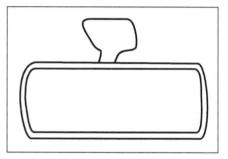

The centre mirror shows you what is directly behind you and also gives you the best view of the vehicle, driver and passengers directly behind your car. It enables you to assess how close the following vehicle is, whether they are slowing down when you are braking, and whether they are fully concentrating and aware of you and your vehicle – not distracted by their mobile phone, drinking, or holding a piece of paper in their hand and aware of you and your vehicle.

RIGHT-HAND SIDE DOOR MIRROR

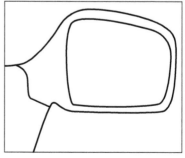

The right-hand side mirror shows you who is on the right-hand side of your car, which may not necessarily be clear in your centre rear-view mirror. It allows you to be aware of anyone overtaking you, or whether it is safe to move your vehicle to the right. In slow or stationery traffic motorcycles and bicycles may approach the front of the queue by riding up on the right-hand side of your vehicle.

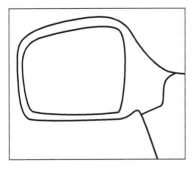

LEFT-HAND SIDE DOOR MIRROR

The left-hand side mirror shows you who is on the left-hand side of your car, which may not necessarily be clear in your centre rear-view mirror. It will help you to be aware of anyone passing you on your left, or whether it is safe to move your vehicle to the left. In slow or stationery traffic bicycles, often approach the front of the queue by riding up on the left-hand side of your vehicle.

Many years ago one of my pupils was on his driving lesson an hour before sitting his driving test.

We had just successfully reversed into a side road and he had got the car ready to move off forward. He checked the mirrors and was about to move off without checking his blind spot. So just as he was about to move off I said *'what about the cyclist?'* So he quickly checked his blind spot. There wasn't a cyclist there actually, but there could have been.

Now about half an hour later he was on his driving test and was also asked to reverse into a side road. After completing the manoeuvre, he was just about to move off and suddenly thought 'cyclist', so checked his blind spot... and sure enough there was a cyclist there which he hadn't seen in either of his mirrors. He successfully kept the car still until the cyclist had safely passed.

My pupil said that he couldn't help smiling when he saw the cyclist because of how I had prompted him earlier, he said that the examiner must have wondered what he was smiling about.

The Blind Spot

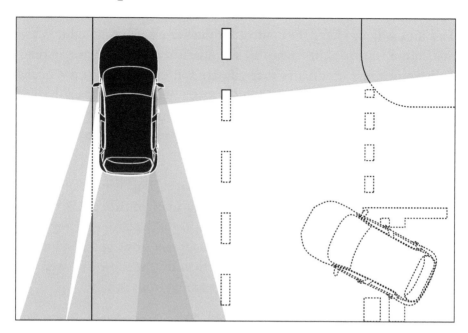

Your 'blind spot' is the area over and slightly behind your shoulder, and is the area not covered by either your side door mirror or centre rear-view mirror. To check it, just turn your head and look over your shoulder – it's just that easy.

I always tell my pupils that sometimes your mirrors will 'lie to you' and tell you that it is safe to move off when, if you had checked your blind spot, you would have realised that it wasn't.

Each and every time you move away from the side of the road or you have any doubts whatsoever, check your blind spot.

Centre Dash Panel

This section will allow you to control all the added extras that your car might offer – your radio station, music player, heaters and air conditioning. Get to know these controls when you are safely parked, and if you have a passenger, encourage them to make any changes while you drive – your attention should always be on the road, looking out for potential hazards, and making safe and sensible decisions.

The heater and fan section is important when you need to demist your windscreen.

This area will also have the control for the hazard warning light. When this button is pressed, it flashes all six indicator lights at the same time. This warns other road-users that you are stationery, and to not queue behind you. Likewise, if you come across someone with their hazard warning lights on, you will need to assess the situation and pass them if it is appropriate to do so. You would normally use your hazard warning lights if you are broken down or forced to stop in a dangerous position.

Alternatively, if you are on a motorway, dual carriageway or on a road with fast flowing traffic, and the vehicles ahead of you are either rapidly slowing or actually coming to a standstill, the hazard warning light warns the traffic behind you that you are not just slowing but stopping. Normally the driver behind you would then do the same and pass the message back along to the drivers approaching from behind.

POWER SOCKETS

Most cars will have one or two power sockets. The one on the left is commonly referred to as a cigarette lighter socket. A few years ago cars came equipped with cigarette lighters and ashtrays. Nowadays we don't have cigarette lighters, just the socket. This socket is very much like the 3-pin electrical wall socket that you have in your home, and this can be used to power electrical accessories, like a car vacuum cleaner, sat nav or a phone charger.

Under the Bonnet

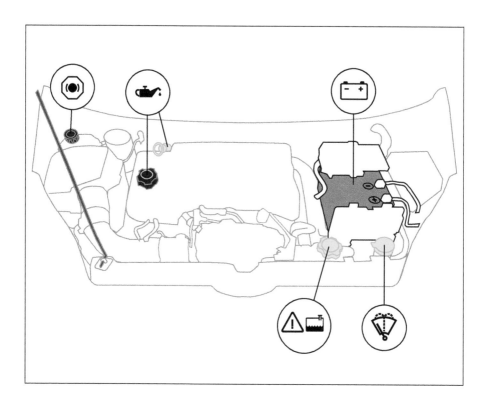

Opening the bonnet

The bonnet release lever on most cars will be inside the front of the car either on the driver's side by your right knee or on the passenger side below the glove box.

When you have pulled the lever, get out and you will see the bonnet has been released and is slightly open. You will then need to look and feel inside the centre of this new gap below the bonnet edge. Find the safety catch and slide it to the left or right to release the bonnet and lift it up: be careful as it may be heavier than you expect, and be especially careful if it is a windy day.

Look for the bonnet 'stay' – a metal stick used to keep the bonnet up – which will lie under the bonnet, on the far right or left of the engine. Insert the stay into the corresponding hole in the underside of the bonnet and the bonnet will then stay up on it's own.

To close the bonnet, you will need to lift it up slightly to release the bonnet stay, and then clip the bonnet stay into it's holder again. You now lower the bonnet to about 6-12cm and allow it to drop. If it doesn't close completely, then just push firmly down on the edge of the bonnet until it lines up smoothly with the rest of the bodywork of the car.

Ignition and battery

To start the engine of a car you need to turn the key in the **ignition**. This is like when you are asleep and someone comes along and gently prods you to wake you up.

BATTERY:

The car **battery** is basically the 'heart' of your car, and without the battery to power the electrical components your car will not start and cannot be driven anywhere.

You will know if you have a problem with your battery if the engine struggles to start when you turn the key in the ignition. It could be that the battery is worn out and needs replacing, or it could be that there is a fault with the alternator, or other component, which keeps the battery charged.

The battery is kept charged when it is being driven – by the alternator on modern cars and by the dynamo on older cars. These components are driven by a belt from the engine.

The car battery also provides electricity to the various electrical components of the car such as the lights, windscreen wipers, heater, audio equipment and so on.

Oil

The **oil** in the car is to ensure that the moving parts of the engine are well lubricated, and so don't cause friction and get too hot. Oil allows these parts can move quickly without melting or welding together causing a 'seized engine'. When you have a 'seized engine' it will be beyond repair and you will need to replace it with a new one. To ensure that this doesn't happen, you should regularly check your oil level - at least once a week.

To do this, open the bonnet of your car and find the dipstick, which will normally have a bright yellow plastic ring on the top. When you pull the dipstick out it will be covered in oil. You will need to wipe this clean with a paper towel or cloth. You then push the dipstick firmly back into the hole you took it from, and then pull it out again. You will then see that there are two marks on the dipstick showing 'maximum' and 'minimum' and the oil level should be showing somewhere between these two marks. If the level is below the minimum mark you will need to top up with some oil. If this is the case, just put in a little at a time and wait for a few moments and then check the level again using the dipstick until the level shows between 'maximum' and 'minimum'.

Radiator

Remember your temperature gauge? As the car is being driven the engine gets warmer – and that's what your temperature gauge is showing you. Just like you if you were to go for a walk or run, the engine will get warmer as it is driven. Your car also has a radiator which contains water to help to keep the engine cool. To keep yourself cool your body will start to sweat, and to replace that fluid you would need have a drink. Just the same, you need to keep putting water in the radiator to keep the engine cool. If the engine isn't kept cool, it will overheat and could result in serious damage to the engine. Always top up or replace your radiator coolant before you drive, and with a cold engine.

Windscreen washer reservoir

You will find your windscreen washer reservoir in the engine compartment. It will normally have a yellow plastic cap with a symbol of the windscreen and wiper on the top. You can top this up at home, or at the 'air and water' area in a petrol station, where drivers check their tyre pressures.

It is very important – and a legal requirement – to keep your windscreen washer bottle topped up with water and ideally a windscreen washer additive. The additive will help remove the more stubborn stains like dead insects or bird droppings.

Hydraulic fluid

During your test you could be asked how would you check the 'hydraulic fluid', or the 'brake & clutch' fluid.

This fluid operates under high pressure and at high temperature, and is needed to ensure that your brakes and clutch work when you press them.

Very often you will find that the hydraulic fluid tank is a plastic tank just in front of the steering wheel. You will see a minimum and maximum mark on the side of the plastic hydraulic container, so you need to ensure that the level is between these two marks.

The levels should be checked weekly and if you are any doubts, contact an experienced mechanic or take it to your local garage.

Tyres

In order to be safe, your tyres need to be at the right pressure, and have the correct tread depth.

To check the tyres have sufficient tread depth and that their general condition is safe to use on the road, you should ensure there are no cuts or bulges, and that there is a minimum of at least 1.6mm of tread depth across the central 3/4 of the breadth of the tyre and around the entire outer circumference.

It is important to regularly check your tyre pressures as this can affect the handling of your car and also prematurely wear out your tyres, requiring them to be replaced. The information for the tyre pressure for your particular car can be found in the manufacturer's handbook.

You can buy your own tyre pressure gauge and tyre inflator or go to your local garage or petrol station where they often will have a tyre pressure machine. Sometimes this can be done for free, others you will need to put a coin or token into the machine for a limited amount of time. If this is the case, you should fully prepare first. If you are going to check all of your tyres (including your spare) you should first remove all the valve caps. Now these will be very dirty, so you could go over to the fuel pumps and get yourself a pair of the free plastic gloves from the dispenser.

The tyre pressure machines can vary. Some will have the pressure number displayed on the machine where you press a '-' or '+' button to set the tyre pressure you require, and some will have a hand gauge where you can read the tyre pressure as you inflate your tyre. Next, you should insert your coin or token, bearing in mind that you have a limited amount of time to complete your task.

Most airlines are fully retracted into the machine so that you will need to pull them out to reach your tyre. Now, you need to firmly push the end of the airline over the tyre valve: you may hear a little bit of air escaping, but when you have got the airline on firmly you will no longer hear any air escaping. Now pull the lever on the hand gauge until you reach the required tyre pressure, or if it is the machine with the display, hold the airline on until you hear the machine 'beep'. When removing the airline, pull the line off squarely and quickly so that you don't lose too much air, otherwise you will have to carry out the procedure again.

When you have successfully checked and inflated your tyres, remember to replace all of the tyre valve caps.

Lights

Any car is fitted with a number of lights that are used to inform other drivers of your intentions when driving:

HEADLIGHTS

Help you see where you are going and allow others to see you.

> To switch your headlights from dipped to full beam, pull your indicator lever towards or away from you and check the blue full beam warning light.

SIDE LIGHTS

These are basically parking lights and should be used when pulled up or parked in an unlit or poorly-lit road after dark.

BRAKE LIGHTS

Ensure that road users behind you are aware that you are braking and therefore reducing speed.

INDICATOR LIGHTS

How other road users are informed of your intention to turn, or change your road position.

HAZARD LIGHTS

These flash all 6 six indicator bulbs at the same time and are used to warn other road users that you are stopped, broken down or that there is a serious danger ahead.

FOG LIGHTS

Some cars are fitted with front and rear fog lights, some only with rear fog lights. Front fog lights light up the road immediately in front of your car as well as alerting oncoming traffic to your presence. You should only use rear fog lights when visibility is less than 100 metres. As a guide, if you're finding it difficult to see the car in front, then the chances are that traffic behind you will find it difficult to see you ahead of them. It is an offence to use your rear fog lights if visibility is better than 100 metres, because not only can they dazzle the driver behind, but they make it more difficult to see your brake lights.

Fuel

To fill your car with fuel, you will need to go to a petrol station. It is helpful if you know which side of your car that your fuel cap is on. On modern cars you will find this information on your fuel gauge where there will be an icon of a fuel pump: beside this fuel pump you will notice a little arrow pointing either to the left or to the right. Whichever way the arrow is pointing is the side that your fuel filler cap is on. It makes sense to park by the pump with your fuel cap nearest to it, but nowadays many garages have extra long fuel hoses, so if there isn't a pump on the ideal side for you, you can always stop with the fuel cap on the far side from the fuel pump.

To fill your car with fuel you will need to follow these steps:

1. Drive up to the pump and stop with your fuel tank nearest to the fuel pump.

2. Open your fuel filler cap – often there will be a little lever you need to pull while you are still in the car. This is normally on the floor next to driver's seat, next to the driver's door.

3. When you leave the car make sure that you lock the doors so that no one can enter or steal anything.

4. Go to where your fuel filler cap is and take the fuel cap off first.

5. Check whether your car uses petrol or diesel, this is often shown on the fuel filler door or in the car owners manual. Do not use the wrong fuel – if you do, call a mechanic or roadside assistance straight away – do not attempt to drive the car, as this will make it much more difficult and expensive to fix.

6. Now check the selection of fuels and select the fuel nozzle for the specific fuel for your car.

7. When you lift the fuel nozzle out of it's holder, hold it upright so that the fuel nozzle is pointing upwards to ensure that you don't spill any fuel over yourself.

8. Push the nozzle about halfway into the fuel tank opening, being careful not to knock the fuel nozzle against the paintwork of your car.

9. Check that the fuel counter and price display windows are showing zero – you may have to wait a few seconds.

10. Now squeeze the movable handle on the fuel nozzle and proceed to fill your fuel tank.

11. When your fuel tank is nearly full, the moveable handle on the fuel lever will loosen and the display of the amount of fuel and cost will stop. You can continue to top up to the nearest pound or litre by squeezing the moveable handle very gently until you reach the required amount.

12. When you take the fuel nozzle out of the fuel tank, be sure to point the fuel nozzle upwards so that you don't spill any fuel on yourself or your shoes, and that you don't spill any on the fuel filler cap which you are going to have to pick up and return to the filler opening.

13. Return the fuel hose to the fuel pump ensuring that the handle locks back into the hook(s) on the pump.

14. Check which pump number you have filled your car from and the amount you are going to pay.

15. Go to the cashier and tell them which pump you used and pay.

16. When you return to your car it is a good idea to make sure that your fuel gauge now registers the fact that you have filled up with fuel.

Legal obligations

Licence

Vehicle Tax and Motor Insurance

MOT and servicing

Licence

Before you learn to drive you'll need to get a valid provisional driving licence. The earliest age you have a driving licence is 17, unless you're registered disabled and can have a provisional driving license at the age of 16.

To get your first provisional driving licence for a car, motorcycle or moped you must:

be a resident of Great Britain - there's a different service in Northern Ireland

meet the minimum age requirement

meet the minimum eyesight requirement

not be prevented from driving for any reason

pay the current fee by card

have a valid UK passport or other form of identity

have your National Insurance number

be able to provide addresses where you've lived over the last 3 years

You can apply for a provisional driving licence when you're 15 years and 9 months old, and you can start driving when you're 17 if you want to drive a car, and 16 if you want to ride a moped or light quad bike.

Visit: **www.gov.uk/apply-first-provisional-driving-licence**

In order to drive legally with a provisional licence, you need to have a car which is road worthy, display red L plates on the front and back, and the driver who accompanies you must be at least 21 years old and have held a full licence for at least three years. The accompanying driver is under the same legal obligations as if they were driving themselves, and so must be within the legal drink drive limit and not using a mobile phone.

As a driver, if you commit any motoring offences you can get points added to your driving licence. Drivers with a full licence who have been driving for more than two years can get up to 12 points on their driving licence before being banned from driving. Bans can be indefinite, or for a certain period of time, which will be decided by a court.

As a new driver, if you get 6 points within the first two years of passing your driving test, you will get an automatic ban and revert back to the beginning again: you will have to buy a new provisional driving licence, take and pass your theory test, and then take and pass your practical test.

You can get points for many offences, the most common being speeding, which can get you between 3-6 penalty points.

Others include:

Failing to stop after an accident **5-10 penalty points**

Careless driving **3-9 penalty points**

Dangerous driving **3-11 penalty points**

Causing death **3-11 penalty points**

Defective vehicle **3 penalty points**

Drink or drug driving **3-11 penalty points**

Traffic signs compliance **3 penalty points**

Using a mobile phone at the wheel **6 penalty points**

Tailgating **3 penalty points**

Not keeping to the left lane on a motorway or dual carriageway

3 penalty points

This is a useful link to be familiar with: **www.gov.uk/penalty-points-endorsements/endorsement-codes-and-penalty-points**

Vehicle Tax and Motor Insurance

When you own a car you are legally required to ensure that it is roadworthy and safe, that it is insured and taxed, and if your car is three years or older, has a current MOT certificate.

It is a legal requirement to have your car insured **before** you drive it. If you get stopped by the police and you're not covered by insurance, you're going to start accumulating points before you've even got your full licence.

You can search online for various insurance comparison websites to find a price that you can afford. Many insurance companies offer monthly payments to make it easier for you to budget.

There are three types of insurance you can purchase: Third Party, Third Party Fire & Theft and Fully Comprehensive.

Third Party is very minimum basic insurance as required by law. This will cover any damage that you may cause to someone else's vehicle or property, but doesn't the cost of repairs to your own vehicle, meaning that you would have to pay for your own damage out of your own pocket.

Third Party, Fire & Theft has the same cover as Third Party but also covers you for damage if your car is stolen or burnt.

Fully Comprehensive covers all of the above but also protects you if your car is damaged.

It's important to inform the insurance company first if you are planning to learn using someone else's car. If you buy your own car, you will need to be clear with the insurance company that it's for a learner driver: there will be an extra premium and these days, insurance companies are very rigorous about knowing that there are changes in circumstances.

After your first 12 months driving with a full licence, as long as you've made no claims, you'll find that your insurance premiums will start to come down dramatically.

MOT and servicing

A car that is three years old or older is legally required to have an annual MOT test. This is carried out by an MOT registered garage. The MOT is to ensure that your vehicle is safe, legal and roadworthy, and will inspect, among other things, your lights, screen, wipers, tyres and brakes.

There is a great difference between getting an MOT for your car and getting your car serviced. When your car is serviced, besides a general check of the overall condition of your car, fluids such as oil, brake & clutch fluid, screen wash and anti-freeze are changed or topped up, and air and oil filters are changed. On a major service other items such as the timing belt and spark plugs will also be changed.

It is advisable to have your regularly serviced normally between 6,000 and 12,000 miles, or at least once a year. Although this isn't a legal requirement, it will help to avoid breakdowns and reduce the risk of getting stranded in the middle of nowhere.

Martin Caswell

Testing

Theory test

Practical

Theory test

The theory test is in two parts, and consists of a series of 50 questions, and fourteen video clips on hazard perception.

The questions have multiple choice answers. Sometimes you'll be asked to select from the four or five possible answers, but very often it's one.

Be aware that the questions in the theory test can cover anything and everything, even vehicles which you may not be intending to drive. It will cover motorway driving even though you may not have driven on a motorway at that point. They may even ask you things maybe about trams or automatic cars, even though you're driving a manual.

Motorway driving for learner drivers came into effect on 4th June 2018 but only in a car fitted with dual controls and with a fully qualified DVSA Approved Driving Instructor.

To prepare for the theory test, your starting point should be to get a recent and up-to-date copy of the Highway Code and actually read it! Lots of people don't read the Highway Code now because there are so many apps and websites on the subject. This is a mistake: get a copy and study it!

There are numerous theory test practice websites and most driving instructors will have links on their websites. Although the actual test is 50 questions, on a lot of sites they are broken down into blocks of 10 to make it easier to learn.

If you are using online tools, try to visualise what would you do if you were on the road, or what would you do if you were in a driving lesson. Think what would your parents do in that situation, or what would your instructor say to you in that situation? This may well help you to eliminate a couple of the answers.

HAZARD PERCEPTION

With the video clips, it's about hazard perception. You've got to be very careful not to do just regular clicks because if you just click every two seconds, the computer will think you are guessing and you will score zero.

If you're very good at hazard perception you will see the hazard well *before* it becomes a hazard. For instance, if on the video you are driving along the road and see a car coming down a side road with a give way sign in front, you might click because that car *might* pull out. If you do, however you wont get the credit for that click, and also risk scoring zero.

Instead one of my pupils came up with the idea that every time you feel the need to brake or turn the steering wheel, that's when you should click. That car coming down the side road is not a hazard yet, so when it begins to emerge or stops just over the line, that's when you need to click, because that's when you would feel the need to brake or turn the steering wheel. To a certain extent, it's more of a hazard **reaction** test than perception.

Can I start driving lessons before passing my Theory Test?

Yes, you can, and it is advisable that you should, as the practical experience will help you understand the questions and answers contained in the theory test. Likewise what you study for the theory test will be very helpful in your practical lessons. You cannot apply for the practical test until you have already passed the theory test: you will need to quote the theory test pass certificate number when booking your practical test.

Practical

The practical driving test is intended to show your driving examiner that you can drive safely and competently by demonstrating that:

You are **SAFE** to yourself

You are **SAFE** to other road-users

You have the vehicle you are driving under your **CONTROL**

That you are driving **LEGALLY**

Regardless of what you may have been told by well meaning friends, colleagues or relatives, the examiners <u>do not</u> have a quota. People still cling to outdated myths, such as if the examiner is in a bad mood, takes a dislike to you, or has reached their 'quota' then you're bound to fail; or the myth that 'no-one' passes at the end of the day, week, month or year. These are all completely untrue. This why the examiner will debrief you at the end of your practical driving test, discussing the actual situations that took place and how you dealt with them.

Before booking your driving test you should discuss and seek advice from your driving instructor to ensure that you will be ready and have covered all of the necessary elements to the required standard, and beyond. You will need to have your driving licence, theory test certificate and your driving instructor's ADI numbers, and a valid credit or debit card.

When booking the practical driving test, you will be given the option of different times and days of the week. Would you like your driving test early in the morning. mid-morning or afternoon? Some people prefer to get their driving test over and done with. some prefer to have their test later in the day, the choice is yours.

Bear in mind that whatever is chosen that your instructor will normally pick you up at least an hour before your Driving Test start time. For example, if you book a Driving Test at 8.10am, your driving instructor will probably arrange to meet you at 7.10am.

When you arrive at the driving centre, you'll be directed into the waiting room. At the appointed time, the examiner will come out and call your name.

The first thing they will do is to ask to see your driving license. Next they will ask you to read and sign two declarations. The first declaration is just to say that you are a UK resident. The second declaration is just to confirm that the car is covered by insurance. If it's a driving school car, it will be, but if it's a private car, this will need to be checked with the insurance company. Driving as a learner drive without being added to a policy it could invalidate it.

Next, you will go out into the car park and the examiner will ask you to read a number plate from 20.5 metres away in good day light. If you can read the number plate that's fine. If you're struggling, the examiner would ask you to step a little bit closer and ask you again.

EYESIGHT

You must be able to read (with glasses or contact lenses, if necessary) a car number plate made after 1 September 2001 from 20 metres. You must also meet the minimum eyesight standards for driving, by having a visual acuity of at least decimal 0.5 (6/12) measured on the Snellen scale (with glasses or contact lenses, if necessary) using both eyes together or, if you have sight in one eye only, in that eye. You must also have an adequate field of vision – your optician can test you for this.

Driving test routes involve around 38-40 minutes of driving and may include higher speed dual and single carriageway roads. This will also include approximately 20 minutes of independent driving, while following a sat nav.

You will only be required to perform one manoeuvre, from the list of four: 'Reverse Bay Park', 'Drive Forwards into parking Bay and reverse out again for two car lengths', 'Parallel Park' and 'Park on the right-hand side of the road, reverse back two car lengths and drive back across to the left-hand side of the road'.

An **Emergency Stop** exercise is carried out in one of every three tests.

You will be asked what are called 'Show Me, Tell Me' questions during your practical test, 'Show Me' questions will ask you to show the examiner how to turn something on in the car. The 'Tell Me' just requires an explanation. Some of these questions will be asked before you begin your test, others will be asked whilst you are driving.

The 'Tell Me, Show Me' questions are set questions and two will be chosen by your examiner at random. You don't have to memorise the answers word for word, it is fine for you to give the answers in your own words as long as you can demonstrate your knowledge to the examiner. Even if you get both questions wrong you will not be given a serious fault or failed, so there is no need to get over anxious. It is still very worthwhile learning the answers to these questions because the knowledge will be very useful to you after you have passed your driving test and in the years to come.

Check out the Useful References section at the back of this book to find links to the government website which lists all the specific questions that you might be asked as part of 'Tell Me, Show Me'. Once you have read this book, you should be able to answer all of them!

Any candidates that commit more than 15 driving faults (minors) will fail their driving test. One serious or one dangerous driving fault (major) will also result in a fail.

At the end of the test, examiners will give candidates guidance notes to explain more fully the report form being issued. Your Driving Instructor will be permitted to listen to this de-brief – with your consent – to further assist you with future driving advice.

AUTOMATIC DRIVING LICENCE RENEWAL

This applies to anyone who applied for a provisional driving licence from the 9th August 2004, and successfully passes their driving test. At the end of the driving test, the examiner will retain your provisional driving licence. You will automatically be sent your new, full driving licence directly from the DVLA. You are still entitled to drive as a full licence holder from the moment you have passed and signed the examiners form.

Everything in this section will be covered in full by this book and by your instructor. If there is anything you are not confident on, tell your instructor and make sure you keep practising. You will get there, and you will be able to pass. Just keep trying, and stay relaxed.

Driving Test Fee

The Practical Driving Test fee pays for the Examiner to test your driving skills. For the most up to date test fees please visit: **www.dsa.gov.uk**

Please note, the driving test fee does not cover the use of the car for the test when using a driving instructor's car. Normally you will book the car with your driving instructor for two hours on the day of your test – possibly longer if you are being picked up a greater distance from the driving test centre. This will give you an hour of practice before the test, and the use of the car on the actual driving test.

LEARNING TO DRIVE

Driving Lessons

In the car

On the road

Driving Lessons

CHOOSING A DRIVING INSTRUCTOR

Like with everything, it's good to ask your friends and family and get some recommendations about driving instructors. Maybe check out some websites so you have an idea of what is available in your area.

It is always tempting to choose the cheapest, however, there are other things that you should take into account.

Find out if they are fully qualified or if they are a trainee instructor. Believe it or not, trainee instructors can still take you out for driving lessons even if they haven't yet qualified. They may have had training, they may have passed the first part of their exams, they may even have passed the second part, but only a qualified instructor has the experience of teaching all sorts of different people in all possible situations.

An experienced, qualified instructor can adapt to what you need: they shouldn't be teaching you the same lesson as their last pupil but tailor everything to your specific learning needs.

For the same reasons, find out how much experience they have since qualifying. Depending on your needs, have a look to see if the instructor specialises in teaching nervous drivers, people with disabilities, dyspraxia or autism.

Finally, have a look to see if they have a website or social media account that might provide testimonials or review.

HOW MANY DRIVING LESSONS WILL I NEED?

There is no minimum or maximum amount. It will be largely dependent on your own aptitude and learning ability. This is where taking professional training from a DVSA (Driving and Vehicle Standards Agency) approved driving instructor is the best course of action, particularly if you have little or no previous experience of driving. Those who pass their driving test have had, on average, about 45 hours of professional training combined with 22 hours of private practice. Learners who prepare this way, with a combination of plenty of professional training and plenty of practice, do better in the test.

Although everyone is different and you may well take less lessons than the 'average', it is recommended that you budget for at least two hours/lessons each week. By keeping your lessons frequent, you are more likely to retain more of what you learnt from your previous lesson, and ultimately will probably take fewer lessons than those with similar ability who only take one lesson a week.

WHERE SHOULD I PRACTICE?

When learning to drive it is a good idea to experience all sorts of different roads, so not just the local town or village where you may live, but you will want to drive everywhere. You want to make sure you have experience of driving on country roads and all the hazards you may come across there, from tractors and trailers to single track roads with passing places. You need to be ready to give-way or to anticipate what the oncoming vehicle is going to do. Maybe they are going to give-way to you, maybe not. Other potential hazards include horses, the big 4x4s or even a herd of cows crossing the road! You need to experience all of them at first hand.

If you live in a small town it's a good idea to go to the nearest big city and experience what it's like to drive there. Get familiar with main roads and faster roads like A roads and dual carriageways.

Dual-carriageways, where the traffic is moving a lot quicker, will also give you some experience overtaking in using slip roads to enter and exit the dual-carriageway. It's sometimes a good idea to pull into lay-bys just to get some practice in reducing your speed coming into the lay-by, being aware of other vehicles parked there, and then afterwards emerging from that lay-by safely enter the traffic flow again.

If your instructor tends to only stay in one particular area, ask them and they will probably be quite happy to take you on all sorts of different of roads. With my pupils in particular I've always made sure that we cover everything so that when they pass the test and begin driving on their own, can say to themselves 'I've done this before'.

Don't necessarily copy the actions of the more experienced qualified drivers around you. You should decide what course action you need to take, and that should always be the safest and most appropriate action for the circumstances.

Many 'qualified drivers' are driving complacently or are not so concerned with driving correctly, safely or attentively – although of course they should be. Many are almost proud to say that if they were to take their driving test again, they would probably fail. The driving test is just a basic test of the drivers' safety to other road users and control of their vehicle, so surely the experienced, qualified driver should be displaying this in their own driving too.

Many qualified drivers will tell you that you only really learn to drive after you have passed your driving test. This is no longer the case, as DVSA approved driving instructors are encouraged to teach their students to drive safely and competently and to fit in with the traffic flow. After passing the driving test, many drivers get sloppy and careless instead of striving to improve their driving skills, and they don't end up 'really learning to drive', but 'learning to crash'.

WHAT TO EXPECT FROM YOUR FIRST LESSON

When you get into the car for the very first time with a driving instructor they will go through the 'cockpit drill' (p61) and all of the controls with you. They will explain how to start the car, the use of the pedals and all the gears. It is likely you will begin to learn clutch control and how to move off straight away. Each instructor will be different, and it is okay to talk to them about how you learn best, and what you are hoping to achieve.

I always tell my pupils that the first 10 minutes of any driving lesson is the 'warm up' time. Likewise, the last 10 minutes tend to be the best.

This, incidentally, is why driving instructors recommend that you have at least an hour driving lesson just before your driving test. By the end of the driving lesson you're warmed up and ready to perform at your best.

ATTITUDE

You are in charge

Treat the car like a naughty child, and it's trying to do things that you don't want it to do. You're the boss, you're not going to let it get away with anything that you haven't agreed to.

Mistakes

If you allow yourself to dwell on your mistake(s) you will go on to make even more, which will ultimately damage your confidence. What is done, is done. You can't change history. Even if you were to drive perfectly for the rest of your life, you have still made mistakes up to this point. Learn from them, rather than dwell on them.

Ask yourself just <u>two</u> questions if you do make a mistake:

What **did** I do?
What **should** I have done?

There is a time and place to reflect on any of your errors, however, and it's not whilst you are still driving in traffic. Keep focused on what you are doing at that moment in time. Be like a dog and live in the present – don't dwell on what happened a few moments ago or what will happen in a few moments time.

Rules

There are no rules that are just rules: you do everything for a reason. The rules of driving are just reasons. Do you look both ways before crossing a road because the Highway Code tells you to do this, or because you don't want to get knocked down?

Decision making

A phrase I often use with my pupils is 'If it's worth thinking about, it's worth doing'. Don't underestimate your ability when considering taking an action like braking, changing gear or signalling. Be careful not to fall into the trap of thinking 'I thought of doing that, but it's probably the wrong thing to do'. As you gain more driving experience and practice, you will get better at judging when to take action.

> ## Be decisive
>
> When driving you need to be very decisive, so drive at a speed where you are thinking faster than you're driving. This way you can always be sure of your next intention.
>
> All the time that you are driving you are trying to predict what the other road-users are doing around you. Likewise, those other road-users are trying to predict what you are going to do next: if you don't know what course of action you are going to take next, how can others predict accurately what you are going to do?

Positivity

When driving, think about what you **do** want to happen, or what you want the car to do, rather than what might happen if you get things wrong. You should concentrate on the 'positive' outcome you do want and not what you don't want.

Trust your instincts. If you think that you need to do something, then you probably do. If a little light came on the dash panel every time to tell you: to brake, to accelerate, to signal, to change gear, to change lane or to check the mirror etc, would you take action then? Every time that something pops into your head, look at that thought as the little light on the dash panel telling you that you need to take that action now. You will reach a point in your driving that nine times out of ten, your instinct will be the correct one.

Experienced drivers tend to drive more on instinct. You need to practise doing the same.

Bullies

Qualified drivers who toot their horn at learner drivers!!! I just want to knock on their heads and ask *'is there anybody in?!'* Everyone had to learn to drive once – yes, even I had to learn to drive and I still remember what it feels like.

There are lots of idiot drivers on the road and we can't always be sure quiet where they are. But when they toot their horn at us in effect they are saying *'I'm the idiot driver and I am sitting in the vehicle right behind you!'*

And finally

Whilst driving, whatever action you intend to take or actually take, imagine that you're 'following yourself".

- Would **'you'** know what the other **'you'** is intending to do?

- Have you made it clear?

- Have you warned and informed other road users of your intentions?

- Is it appropriate and safe to take this action?

In the car

COCKPIT DRILL

Every time you get into the car you should carry out the following:

Door: Ensure your door is securely closed

On most cars there is a courtesy light by the centre rear-view mirror. When the doors are closed this light should go off. If the light is still on, it probably means that one of the doors.

Seat: Adjust your seat (and steering wheel if necessary)

Adjust your seat so you can reach the pedals and push the clutch pedal all the way to the floor comfortably, without stretching or feeling cramped. Most cars have adjustments on the seat, allowing you to move forward, backward, change the angle of the backrest and so on.

The head restraint should be adjusted so that the rigid part is at least as high as the eye or top of the ears, and as close to the back of the head as is comfortable.

N.B. Some restraints might not be adjustable.

Mirrors: Adjust your centre mirror and your side mirrors

Ideally, the centre mirror will show as much of the back window as possible. When you adjust the centre interior mirror, hold the outer frame of the mirror so that you avoid putting finger marks on the glass. When adjusting the side mirrors, ensure that you can see just a small part of the edge of your car in each, but most of the road.

Belt: Put your seat belt on

Make sure it's not twisted, it's not uncomfortable, and make any adjustments that you need to make.

Handbrake: Ensure that the handbrake is on

Make sure the handbrake has been pulled up and that the warning light is telling you it is on.

Gearstick: Ensure that the gear lever is in the neutral position

Check the gear lever is in neutral by moving it from side to side. If it's in gear it will move a little bit, if it's in neutral it will move a lot from left to right.

Door, seat, mirrors, belt, handbrake, gearstick: If you adjust your mirrors before you have adjusted your seat, you'll have to do so again when you move position. Do these things in this order and you will find that you won't have to repeat any of them.

BASICS

Remember the first 'Rule of the Road' is to 'Keep to the left', unless you can think of a very good reason why you shouldn't. Each time you need to move away from the left-hand side of the road, think about when and how soon you should return to the left again. If you're not sure, keep to the left anyway.

This also goes for the position of your vehicle on the road - always position it closer to the left, rather than using the centre of the road as your guide for positioning.

Remember that you carry a spare wheel, but you don't carry a spare front wing!

Never beckon to other road users – drivers, riders, pedestrians - to proceed but allow them to make their own decision. The only vehicle that you can control is the one that you're in. If you should beckon someone to proceed and this results them being involved in an accident, they will apportion some or all the blame on you for saying that it was safe for them to proceed.

POM POM

POM stands for Prepare, Observe, Manoeuvre. POM POM is fun to say, and easy to remember.

Prepare: get the car completely ready to move off

Observe: look and assess if is it safe and clear to proceed

Manoeuvre: move your car - proceed with the manoeuvre

When you stop at traffic lights, road junctions, roundabouts or for approaching traffic to pass by, always immediately prepare your car ready to move off again. Always 'prepare' first, before you 'observe'. While you're observing and an opportunity presents itself, allowing you to proceed, if you're not ready by the time you have 'prepared', another road-user will have arrived, now preventing you from proceeding.

How to prepare:

Look at this another way. If as a pedestrian with four heavy bags and you wanted to cross the road from one pavement to the pavement on the other side of the road, what would you do first?

Would you observe and wait for a gap in the traffic and then pick up heavy bag number one, then observe again and pick up bag number two, then observe again and pick up bag number three, observe again and then pick up bag number four? No, of course you wouldn't, because the opportunity to have crossed the road would have been missed.

In reality you would pick up all four of your heavy bags first, and then observe for a gap in the traffic, and when the opportunity comes you would cross the road.

So when intending to move off from the side of the road, at a junction or a roundabout your four bags will be:

❶ Clutch down to the floor

❷ Select 1st gear

❸ Set gas and find the 'bite point' of the clutch

❹ Hand on the handbrake, ready to release

MSM

MSM stands for Mirror, Signal, Manoeuvre.

Mirror: Know what is behind and beside you. You should check the mirror in pairs: When you are about to move your car to the right, you should check your centre rear-view mirror and your right-hand side door mirror, and when you are about to move your car to the left, you should check your rear-view mirror and your left-hand side mirror.

Signal: Make clear your 'intention' to move your car to a different road position. Not that you are going to move, but that you would like to move your car to a different road position. You are 'informing other road users of the action you are preparing to take.

Manoeuvre: Establish that it is now safe to carry out your intended change of road position by checking your mirrors again to observe how the following road users have reacted to your signal and then complete the change of road position.

Use MSM whenever you are about to change your vehicle road position, turning at a road junction or roundabout.

MIRRORS

Check your mirrors frequently. Check your mirrors **before** and **after** you do anything. Remember: You cannot 'wear out' your mirrors.

One wise man from the Institute of Advanced Motorists said words to the effect:

'Never place your vehicle somewhere that your eyes haven't visited first!'

Particularly check your mirrors:

Before and after you change your speed

Before and after you change your road position

It's like you're taking photographs and you're trying to spot the difference between the two pictures you've just taken. When the pictures are clear and not changing, you are then in a position to take the appropriate action to keep yourself and other road-users safe.

SIGNALS

When should you use a signal? – When there are any **'eyeballs'** to see it!

Consider, are there any other road users, including cyclists and pedestrians who may benefit from knowing what you are intending to change your road position or complete a turn at a roundabout or road junction? If so, use your signal so that you will not cause any problem to anyone else and they are less likely to cause you any problem either.

The use of signals, or indicators, are not to inform of what you are **going** to do immediately, but of what you **intend** to do when a safe opportunity presents itself.

If you signal and move immediately, other road users may not have time to react to your intentions.

It normally takes around 3 to 5 flashes of the indicator to get another road users' attention, as they may be concentrating on something else, so ensure that you signal in plenty of time before you actually need to change your road position. Therefore, always follow The Highway Code and 'give clear signals in plenty of time...'

Keep the signal on until you have completed whatever manoeuvre you intended to complete, and only cancel your signal when you have completed the manoeuvre in its entirety. If you cancel your signal just before you complete your manoeuvre, it could look as if you have changed your mind, and that you are now about to go in a completely different direction.

Think of a person you know who deliberately or obstinately 'gets hold of the wrong end of the stick', or is just being awkward to make a point. This is the person who could be watching your signal and jump to the wrong conclusion, involving you or others in an accident.

So, when changing lanes, keep your signal on until you have got all your wheels in the new lane. If you cancel your signal when you are partially in the lane, it could give the other road-users the impression that perhaps you have changed your mind and are returning to your original lane position.

When leaving a roundabout and signalling your intention just before the exit you intend to take, keep the signal on until you have completely left the roundabout.

If you cancel the signal just before you leave, it could give the impression that you have changed your mind and are perhaps going to leave at the following exit.

MOVING OFF FROM STANDSTILL

As you move off, use your accelerator (gas) pedal and clutch pedal in a see-saw motion, so that as you press the accelerator down, you are allowing the clutch to come up, moving the pedals simultaneously. Stalling is caused by bringing the clutch up too quickly, without sufficient gas, or a combination of both. This point at which the car goes from stationery to moving as a result of your pedal action is called the 'bite point'.

As you allow the clutch come up, causing the car to move, the gas needs to be increased to take up the weight of the car, thus preventing the stall.

If your focus is elsewhere, you are less likely to move safely and under full control. Don't let the fact that there is traffic surrounding you to distract you. Just keep in mind that the car doesn't know where you are, it's just a mechanical object.

While you're concentrating on moving off, you're not distracted by the amount of traffic. Likewise, while you're focused on the amount of traffic around you, you're no longer concentrating on moving off under control.

Some of my pupils say that they would rather be riding their horse. But I explain when riding you have two sets of emotions to control, yours, and the horse's. **You** may be in full control but if the horse sees or hears a loud noise, you can be out of control in a second. When driving, you just need to keep your own emotions under control, and then you have the car under your control.

The quickest way to move off is to move off slowly! If you rush your actions, you will not be so accurate.

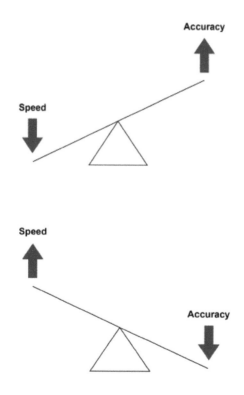

The 'Magic 3-Seconds'

When moving off, for example, you are much more likely to stall the engine if you try to move quickly, rather than by taking your time. If when moving off from standstill you hold the clutch still when you reach the 'bite point' and the car just begins to move, **hold** the clutch very still for 3 seconds by counting out loud or in your head 1, 2, 3 and then you can allow the clutch to come all the way up to the top. By doing this each time you move off, the car will never jerk or stall. This is what I refer to as the 'Magic 3-seconds'. Remember that the car is mechanical and has no emotions, unlike a dog or horse and will not 'play you up' irrespective of the traffic conditions you are in at the time.

But if you bring the clutch up to the 'bite point' and then immediately allow it to come all the way up to the stop it will almost always result in a jerk or more likely a stalled engine. By the time you've stalled the engine and restarted this will have taken considerably longer and take at least 10 seconds – compared to moving off slowly taking just 3 seconds – or even longer.

Imagine 'Balance Scales'. On one side you have 'Speed' and on the other side 'Accuracy'. When the Speed goes up, the Accuracy comes down. How do you increase the Accuracy? By reducing the Speed. As you slow the Speed of your action, the Accuracy improves.

This is not just applicable to driving, but to whatever you do at home, at work etc. Consider something that you did really well. It probably took a while to complete. Then consider something that you did poorly. It probably didn't take long at all.

Whatever actions you are about to take, 'Don't Rush'!

Remember to always balance **'Accuracy'** versus **'Speed'**

When you stall whilst moving off from a junction, roundabout or traffic lights etc, the first instinct is to look in the mirror to see how the following driver is reacting.

By all means have a quick glance, but certainly don't dwell on their reaction. Instead, fully focus and concentrate on moving off slowly and carefully under control to ensure that this time you will not stall again.

Just for a moment put yourself in the place of the following driver after you have stalled. So the driver in front of you has just stalled. Do you want the driver of car that has just stalled to be staring at you wondering how you are going to react, or do you just want the driver in front of you to re-start the engine and concentrate fully on moving off successfully?

You may well misjudge the reaction of the following driver in any case. Even if you think that they are shouting or ranting at you, they may just be singing along with their music, chatting via Bluetooth or even in deep conversation with their passengers.

BE READY

Hold on to the handbrake when you see a possible opportunity to move off. Don't wait until it is clear before you get ready as you will most likely miss your opportunity to move off. If you're about to leave the house and you just want to finish your cup of tea first. Would you pick it up and take a sip, put it down on the table, pick it up again and take another sip, then put it down on the table again, then pick it up again? You see what I'm getting at now. You should be completely **prepared** and **ready** to go **now,** so that when the opportunity arises for you to move off you just need to release the handbrake and go.

STOPPING AND SLOWING DOWN

When asked to pull up and stop at the side of the road, firstly check your mirrors to be aware of anyone behind you. Next, when deciding where to stop your car, consider 'Best' place and 'Worst' place to stop, rather than just stopping randomly. Where you choose to stop should cause other road users the least inconvenience. There is always one place that is going to be better or worse than the other.

When reducing your speed by either slowing down or coming to a complete stop, concentrate on the driver behind you, initially.

Before considering where you are going to stop your vehicle, concentrate on warning the driver behind you, by using your footbrake, which lights up your rear red brake lights. By getting the following driver's attention and getting them to slow down early, you can then concentrate on stopping safely in the knowledge that the driver behind you is fully aware of your intention to slow down or stop.

Many drivers overlook this technique and solely concentrate on where they are going to stop **before** considering whether the driver behind them is fully focused on the fact that they are slowing down or stopping.

When a driver gets hit from behind they often say '...*there was nothing I could do...*', this is because they were concentrating **only** on where they were intending to stop, without considering whether the driver behind was concentrating and also able to stop safely too.

> **When driving, make a mental profile of the driver behind you, and their style of driving. They might be erratic, too close, talking to passengers, distracted by kids or animals in the car, or they might appear to be fiddling with something as they're driving. Make allowances for what you see – perhaps braking sooner, and softer than normal to get their attention!**

This is why you should also plan to also leave a space in front of you when stopping, so that you can use that space if the following driver is not fully alert, or in an extreme emergency, even swerving around the vehicle in front of you to avoid a collision from the driver behind. Of course, you need to be careful that in changing course you will not be avoiding one accident and getting involved in another!

Stopping

When stopping your car, you will need to brake to initially slow the car down, and then before the car comes to a complete halt, you will need to push the clutch down to the floor.

To stop the car without pushing the clutch down just before it stops, is like when riding your bicycle, and stopping without putting your foot on the ground: you would fall over, or in this case, stall.

> **Many drivers push the clutch down before or at the same time as they push the brake pedal. This is very dangerous and compromises your potential stopping distance.**
>
> **With most modern cars manufactured in the last 30 years or so, you can, and should, leave the pushing down of the clutch until around walking speed or about 5mph, or where you feel the car begin to shudder. This way you will get 100% reduction in your speed from your footbrake.**

With the clutch already down, the brakes only work at about 60% efficiency so the ability to stop quickly is compromised by about 40% compared to keeping the clutch up.

If you had two cars side by side travelling at exactly the same speed and they both braked at exactly the same time with the same amount of pressure, but one driver had the clutch down and the other driver leaves the clutch up until the last moment, the one with the clutch down will have stopped much further forward than the one who delayed pushing the clutch down.

Once you have pulled up to the side of the road or stopped, always do the following:

Handbrake: You put the handbrake on first to ensure that whatever else might go wrong, your car isn't going to stall or roll away.

Select Neutral: so that the car can't stall and so that you can now rest your feet, by removing your feet from the pedals.

Cancel the Signal: Because this is the least of your priorities in relation to the previous two actions. Also, because if you cancel your signal the moment you stop, it gives other the road-users the impression that you may have changed your mind and you are possibly going to move off again. By leaving the signal until last, it will have been on for some time, which confirms that you are intending to stop here.

Slowing down

When driving at 70mph, use the footbrake to reduce your speed, then only push the clutch pedal down for the last 5mph. Likewise if you are travelling at 50mph, down to 5mph, then push the clutch pedal down.

You could argue that it doesn't matter too much around town or at low speed, but it really does matter. The main reason that it matters is because when you develop the habit of delaying putting down the clutch until almost at a standstill, you will also have conditioned yourself to do this at higher speed in greater emergency situations. So even when travelling at 30mph, lose the first 25mph, then push the clutch down for the final 5mph.

Stopping Distance

2-4-10 – Only A Fool Breaks The 2 Second Rule

You may have heard the above saying 'Only a fool breaks the 2 second rule'. But what does it mean?

When you are following another vehicle, you should be **at least** 2 seconds behind it, but preferably more. This is applies when driving on dry roads.

On wet roads this should be doubled to **at least** 4 seconds, as wet roads are obviously more slippery than dry roads. So then you say 'Only a fool breaks the 2 second rule, When it pours make it 4'.

On snow and ice you should keep **at least** 10 seconds back from the vehicle in front.

Unfortunately there are many more accidents on wet roads because although drivers know that it is more slippery in the wet, they still tend to drive at the same distance that they do in the dry! If you were to ask the same driver – before an accident – which do you think you could stop quickest on, a dry road or a wet road, most would laugh at you and say a dry road, but, the same driver doesn't put it into practice. They only realise this when they are about to collide with another vehicle, road user or other obstruction, when they suddenly realise that they should have anticipated and been keeping further back, braked sooner, and adapted to the road and weather conditions.

How do you define a wet or damp road? Sometimes the sun is shining and the skies are blue and it all too easy to ignore or just not notice the fact that the roads are wet or damp. The way I define whether the road is dry or not is by asking the question 'Would you sit on this road?' and 'Would you have a damp patch on your behind?'. If you said you would have a damp patch, then you should keep at least 4 seconds from the vehicle in front.

How do you measure 2 seconds, 4 seconds or 10 seconds? When the vehicle in front of you passes a fixed object such as a road sign, building, Bridge, tree or something similar, it should take you at least 2 seconds (4 or 10 seconds depending on the conditions) to reach that same point.

STEERING

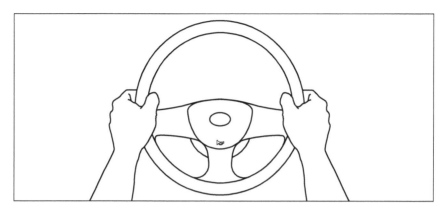

As you know, to keep control of the wheel, you should place your hands at 'quarter to three' or 'ten to two' as if it were a clock face. A lot of learners – myself included when I was learning to drive – try to watch the end of the bonnet to make sure you don't run into anything. In doing so you are no longer looking far enough ahead to make any necessary steering adjustments to keep you on a straight course.

As a pedestrian, do you look at the end of your shoes as you walk along? Of course not, otherwise you would walk into people, into lamp posts and veer off the pavement. Think about where you are looking as you walk along the pavement. You look ahead and are aware of any upcoming hazards and turns.

To keep the car straight as you are driving along, you need to look into the far distance. This will allow you will detect any veering off course much sooner, and enable you to keep the car on a much straighter course.

Where you're looking is where you go.

SPEED AND LIMITS

Remember: It's not how fast you can drive along a particular stretch of road but how quick you can STOP!

Generally, where there are street lights, the speed limit is 30mph, unless it is signed otherwise. Likewise, if there are no street lights, it is normally the national speed limit (60mph on single carriageway and 70mph on a dual carriageway) unless signed otherwise.

When driving in an urban area, if you haven't seen any speed limit signs, look into the side roads. If you notice a 30mph as you drive past the side road, then the road you are on will be a different speed limit. So now you know you need to look for a speed limit sign along the road you are driving, which will be anything other than 30mph.

If the cars behind you appear to be getting smaller and smaller in your mirrors, you are probably exceeding the speed limit!

When changing from one speed limit to another, the speed limit hasn't changed until you reach the new speed limit sign. Just imagine that there is an invisible tape strung across between the two new speed limit signs. You have to burst through the tape before you are in the new speed limit zone.

Now a lot of people tend look at speed limits as targets, particularly young people once they have just passed their driving test and been let 'off the leash'. It says 60, I can drive at 60. Very often I go down country roads on driving lessons and students say, 'what! It's 60 here?' And I say, no that's the upper limit, not the recommended limit.

In the old days we never used to have an upper limit. That white circular sign with a black diagonal line meant 'end of speed limit'. In other words, end of 30 or end of 40 and it means you are allowed to drive a little bit faster if appropriate.

At all times, you want to be driving at an appropriate speed. A speed for the road, traffic and weather conditions.

A lot of people think of accidents being caused by wet roads, ice or snow. In fact, it's always just two words: driver error. It's the drivers not adapting to the conditions. It's not how fast you can drive along a piece of road but it's how quickly you can stop. And that's what you've got to always keep in mind.

ADVERSE WEATHER CONDITIONS

While preparing for the theory test you will have to learn what are the legal distances you should you leave between your car and the vehicle in front.

This isn't just theory, though, it's very important in practice: in dry and good conditions it's two seconds, in the wet conditions it's four seconds, in ice and snow it's 10 seconds.

It's not just the action of being able to stop, it's when you see those brake lights. Unfortunately, the brake lights are exactly the same whether they're braking slightly or performing an emergency stop.

So when you're following a car and you first see those brake lights you must think, are they slowing a little bit or are they performing an emergency stop, are they coming to a standstill?

By the time that you've worked out that they're coming to a standstill if you're within that two second gap, you've probably hit them. So if you're three or four seconds away in dry weather, you've got time to decide. In wet weather if you're five or six seconds, you've got thinking time, in snow or ice 12 or 15 seconds you've got even more thinking time.

Children and Pedestrians

When driving along and you see children running out in front of you, **don't** assume that the ones you now see are the only ones there.

ALWAYS look for the 'next one'.

When you see two children crossing the road, where is the third one? If you see three children crossing the road where is the fourth one? This is particularly important if your view of the road is obstructed or reduced by parked vehicles, buildings or deviation of the road.

In particular, keep in mind, that although you may expect to see an adult walking out between parked cars because you can see movement through the car windows, very young children are much shorter, and may not be visible before they suddenly step out.

Be even more aware when approaching larger vehicles including people carriers, 4x4s, vans, buses and lorries. Be particularly aware when passing a stationary queue of oncoming vehicles where pedestrians and children may consider crossing the road between them.

You ALWAYS need to be driving at such a speed that in the event of an emergency, you can still pull up and stop safely.

WHICH GEAR?

When you first start learning to drive everyone and their dog will tell you that you will know when to change gear, because *'the engine will tell you'*.

I was told this too when I first started learning and remember thinking to myself *'No I won't! How could I possibly just know when the right time would be?'*

Annoyingly, those people were right. You get used to the sound of the engine getting louder, which is a hint that it is time to change up to the next gear. But when you are reducing speed and need to change down to a lower gear, you don't hear any change in the engine sound: you just need to 'know'.

The best rule is:

'if you change your speed, change your gear'

or

'New speed = New gear'.

As a rough guide, many cars you would drive up to 10 miles per hour (mph) in first gear and then change to second gear. As you increase speed to 20mph change to third gear, increase speed to 30mph and change to fourth gear, and then from 40mph plus change to fifth gear.

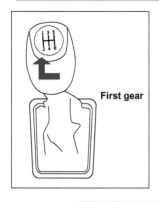

First gear

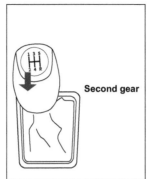

Second gear

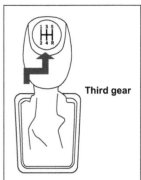

Third gear

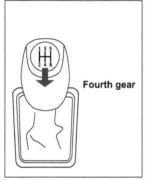

Fourth gear

Fifth gear

By changing up to the next gear, you will help your fuel consumption by not using so much fuel. If you can imagine that your gas (accelerator) pedal is like a tap, the more you press it down, the more fuel you suck out of your fuel tank. So only gently press the gas pedal until you reach the ideal speed for the next gear change, after changing gear you will only need to press the gas pedal a little to reach the ideal speed for the following gear change and so more fuel is used when either the gas pedal is pushed right down or the car is driven much faster than necessary for the gear.

Therefore, even before you start the gear change procedure, think about which gear you are currently in, and which gear you are about to select – and only then – commence the gear change.

You will also need to change gear depending on the steepness of the road you are driving. When driving up a hill, for example, you may well find that the car begins to struggle. Now it may be necessary to change to a lower gear to make it easier, and to help the car climb up the hill.

When you're riding your bicycle you change gear when you're going up a hill to make it easier to get up the hill. If you didn't change gear you would either struggle, or come to a stop. Likewise, if you stayed in the same gear that you used to get up that steep hill when you're now riding on the flat, you would be pedalling furiously but going quite slowly - you would change 'up' to the next gear.

When you're on your bicycle you are the 'engine'. If you don't change gear the 'engine' would struggle or become worn out. Changing gear in your car has the same effect.

Another way to master this is to try to keep the engine relatively quiet. The more noise the more fuel is being used and the more wear and tear on the engine and gearbox. The quieter you drive the more economic it is for you.

Always be:

In the correct gear. At the correct speed. At the correct time.

By ensuring the above, you will always be in full control, and as a consequence be driving safely at all times and ready to respond to any change of situation.

Changing gear

If you were on a bike you were to stop pedalling, just for a moment, the bicycle would quite rapidly start to slow down, as there is no power driving it forward. Therefore, when you change gears, particularly when driving up a slope or hill, the clutch needs to be down only for a very short time, otherwise the vehicle will lose momentum. Whilst the clutch is down, there is nothing driving the car forward, you are in effect free-wheeling, or coasting.

Always put your hand on gear lever first, then put the clutch down, and come off the gas. If you put clutch down before you put your hand on the gear lever, you start to lose momentum (your speed), particularly when going up a hill. Rather like when you get dressed in the morning: Socks on first or shoes on first - every time?! Of course, you always put your socks on first, so it is the same when changing up a gear, it is ALWAYS hand on gear lever, clutch down, off gas.

When changing to a lower gear i.e. from third gear to second gear, instead of bringing the clutch up in one movement, bring it up in two steps. Just bring the clutch up to the 'bite' point, hold for a split second, and then bring it up gently to the top. Even if you are travelling a little too fast for the lower gear, this method will eliminate any jerking as you change to the lower gear.

My driving instructor used to say to me *'imagine your grandmother is sitting in the back of the car drinking a very hot cup of tea!'*

If you find that when changing from second to third gear, you keep ending up in first or fifth gear, don't wrap your hand around the gear lever, but gently nudge the gear lever forward with your hand open, just using your palm. The gear lever is spring-loaded and always wants to line up with third and fourth gear.

Rather like taking a child into a sweet shop and insisting they have some sweets... you don't have to insist... they WANT them!

So don't put any effort into 'pushing' the gear lever forward, but just let it 'fall' into 3rd gear!

Many years ago, in the early days of my teaching career, I was teaching a middle-aged lady to drive. We were driving up a hill in third gear and the car was beginning to struggle. She said to me 'I know that I need to change gear, but do I change to fourth gear or to second gear?'

My reply was 'Imagine that you are walking as a pedestrian and carrying three heavy bags of shopping up this hill, and you are now beginning to struggle with the weight. What would make it easier for you, if someone giving you an extra bag, so that you now have four bags, or if someone takes a bag off you, so that you now only have two bags?'

She then realised, that having only two bags after struggling with three bags would feel much easier. The answer is to change down to a lower gear when your car begins to struggle as it climbs a hill.

FUEL EFFICIENCY

Be careful not to be revving your engine whilst waiting at red traffic lights, pedestrian crossings or busy junctions as this waste's a lot of fuel.

In the current economic climate, fuel is relatively expensive and therefore you don't want to waste any, particularly when you're not even moving along the road.

Visualise your gas pedal like a tap. The more you press it down, the more fuel is sucked out of your fuel tank and more money is sucked out of your wallet!

This also occurs when driving fast, as that requires you to push the gas pedal down further. By driving a little slower, besides being able to observe more, you will also actively reduce your fuel costs.

On the road

CROSSINGS AND TRAFFIC LIGHTS

You **must** obey all traffic lights, even temporary ones.

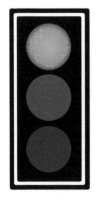 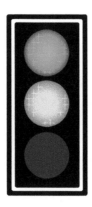 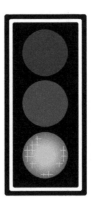 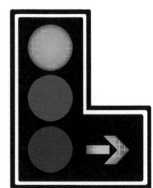

RED light

Means stop behind the stop line. If you move over the stop line while the traffic light is at red you have committed a traffic offence, which carries a fine and three penalty points on your driving licence.

RED and AMBER light:

still means stop, but the traffic light is about to turn to **green**. But don't move too quickly, be sure to check before, and as, you move off, that other vehicles on the road ahead of you are not driving through their **red** traffic lights.

GREEN light:

means that you can go on as long as the way ahead is clear. Just be aware when turning left or right, for any pedestrians or cyclists who may be crossing the road and be ready to give way to them. When turning right, wait for oncoming traffic, and only complete your right turn when the road is clear.

If you have stopped for a red light at the 'stop line' and then the traffic light changes to green, you should move forward to the 'normal position' for turning into a side road on your right. As you move forward you may observe some thin black tarmac strips on the road which look like scars from previous road repairs. But they are in fact traffic light sensors. When you move forward the traffic lights now know that there is a vehicle waiting to turn right. Therefore, if the traffic is very heavy on your road the green traffic light right-turn filter arrow will come on allowing you to proceed with your turning right. Be very careful though of any oncoming traffic still approaching even though they should have stopped as their light changes to red around 3 seconds before your green filter arrow lights up.

If while you have moved forward over the stop line waiting for the opportunity to complete your right turn, the traffic light turns back to red, you are now committed and still need to complete your turn otherwise you will be obstructing emerging traffic from the side road.

RED light with GREEN filter arrow

If the **red** light is shown on it's own you will need to stop. But if the **green** filter arrow comes on for the direction that you want to turn, you can move off, but **only** in the direction of the green arrow.

AMBER light

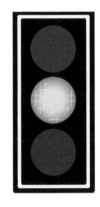

Means that you must **stop** at the stop line. You can continue only if you have already crossed the stop line or if you genuinely feel that you may cause an accident if you were to stop quickly, such as if there is a vehicle too close behind you. Many drivers drive through an **amber** light even though they can easily stop safely because they 'can't be bothered', or they're running late, but this type of behaviour is putting other road users in potential danger. The only exception is where the amber light is flashing, and provided the road is clear and there are no pedestrians crossing or about to cross the road, you can drive on.

PELICAN CROSSING
(Pedestrian Light Controlled Crossing)
Now superseded by the puffin crossing

Pelican crossings are controlled by the pedestrian pressing a button on the WAIT box. Pedestrians should only cross when the green man lights up and all the traffic has stopped. Sometimes there is a bleeper to help blind or partially sighted people know when it is safe to cross. Alternatively, there may be a rotating knob underneath the WAIT box, which turns when the green man lights up. Pedestrians should not start to cross if the green man is flashing. We no longer install pelicans as the newer puffin crossings provide a better facility for pedestrians.

PUFFIN CROSSINGS
(Pedestrian User Friendly Intelligent Crossing)

Puffin crossings look very similar to pelicans and they are an updated version of a pelican crossing. One of the main differences is that the red and green man signals are just above the WAIT box and not on the other side of the road. Pedestrians should still press the button on the box. Puffin crossings have special sensors built in which can detect a pedestrian waiting and make sure that traffic remains stopped until all the pedestrians have crossed the road.

Puffins do not have a flashing green man for pedestrians or a flashing amber for drivers.

TOUCAN CROSSINGS
(**Two Can** Cross)

These crossings are provided for pedestrians and cyclists, usually at sites where cycle routes cross busy roads. They are similar to a puffin, with the crossing operated by a push button on the WAIT box. On a toucan there is a green and red cycle signal as well as the more familiar red and green man.

The main advantage for cyclists is that they do not have to dismount to cross. Toucans also have sensors to detect pedestrians using the crossing.

There is no flashing green man signal and drivers must wait for a green light.

ZEBRA CROSSING

This crossing has black and white stripes (like a zebra) with orange flashing beacons at each end. A zebra crossing gives the pedestrian right of way once their foot is on the crossing. However, pedestrians must make sure that all the traffic has stopped before crossing, and they should keep looking and listening as they cross.

The pedestrian crossing is one of the few times that pedestrians have priority over the motorist or cyclist. When approaching a pedestrian crossing, look well ahead and see if a pedestrian is likely to reach the crossing at the same time as you. If so, be ready to slow down and stop to give way to the pedestrian. You will also need to be very aware of any vehicles behind you and how close they are. If necessary, begin to slow down a little early in order to get the driver behind you to start slowing down.

Even though the pedestrian only has priority once they put a foot on the crossing, some may be quite bold and step onto the crossing as you arrive at it, so it is better to be prepared and ready to stop for the safety of the pedestrian, the following vehicle and yourself.

Many people ask for zebra crossings to be changed to puffin crossings, believing them to be safer. Recent research has shown that the safety record of both types is very similar and that, in some cases, zebras are safer.

ROUNDABOUTS

When going straight ahead at a roundabout from the left lane. Keep well to the left on the roundabout itself to ensure that you don't you don't obstruct the lane on your right. An easier way to ensure that you do this safely and correctly is to move over towards the traffic island as you drive onto the roundabout, and as you reach the traffic island to check your centre and left hand mirror and signal to the left.

An easier way to remember this is to 'Drive over to the traffic island to signal'.

If as you drive over to the left on the roundabout it feels 'Awkward' you've positioned your car well.

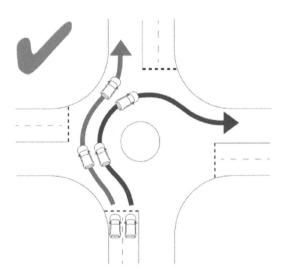

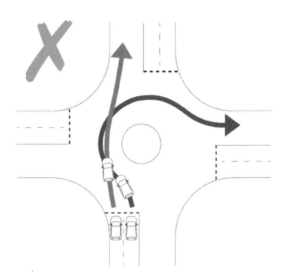

If it feels quite easy, you have probably just 'Straight-Lined' the roundabout and possibly caused any vehicle(s) in the right-hand lane to take evasive action to avoid a collision.

As you approach a roundabout there will be signs that show you the different destinations of each road leading away from it. Because each of these roads are how you leave the roundabout, they are referred to as 'exits'.

The 'first exit' will almost always take you down a road to the left. The 'second exit' is often a road which will take you straight on, or which will continue the road you are already driving on, and the 'third or fourth exit' will most commonly be a road that will take you off to the right.

Of course this is a very rough guide, because some roundabouts won't have a left turn, and the first exit will in fact take you straight on. Other roundabouts might have five or six exits, and so it will not be as simple as going right or left. This is why it's important to take note of the road signs which tell you which road you want to be on, and therefore which exit you need to take.

As you approach the roundabout sign, check the rear view mirror and look at the layout of the roundabout on the road sign. Check for your destination road, and note which exit you need to take.

If you are taking the first exit, or turning left, then you should check the left-hand side mirror, signal to the left, and check the rear view mirror and left-hand side mirror again. Brake to reduce speed to 20mph or less, and position the car in the left hand lane, or to the left of the road approaching the roundabout.

If you are taking the second exit, or turning going straight ahead, then you should check the left-hand side mirror, signal to the left, and check the rear view mirror and left-hand side mirror again. Brake to reduce speed to 20mph or less, and position the car in the left-hand or central lane. If there are more than two lanes, there may well be markings on the road to indicate the lane you need to be in. If you are not certain, stay to the left.

If you are taking the third or fourth exit, or turning right, then you should check the right-hand side mirror, signal to the right, and check the rear view mirror and right-hand side mirror again. Brake to reduce speed to 20mph or less, and position the car in the right-hand lane, or to the right of the road approaching the roundabout.

> When approaching junctions and roundabouts where you are intending to go straight ahead assume that you should take the left lane. The first 'rule of the road' is 'drive on the left'. Your default lane should be the left lane unless you can think of a good reason not to, and while you're thinking of a good reason, stay on the left. It is always going to be easier and safer to move from the left lane to the right, than be in the right lane and try to move over to the left, because of the blind spots of your window pillars and head restraints as you look across to the left.
>
> You have to have a good reason not to drive on the left, such as road signs or road markings telling you to take a different road position.

Assess the roundabout for approaching traffic from the right, and decide whether to proceed or stop. At a roundabout, the vehicle approaching from your right, or approaching from ahead with its right-turn signal on, has priority. You may only proceed as long as you don't cause the driver approaching on your right to brake, swerve or take any avoiding action.

When it is clear, or if it is clear on the approach, continue onto the roundabout. Look into the road that you are turning into for hazards: there might be pedestrians crossing the road, parked vehicles or queuing traffic. If the road is clear, build up your speed and change up to the next gear. Check your rear view mirror, and your left-hand side mirror, and as you pass the exit before the one you intend to take, signal to the left. Check your mirrors again and turn left, off the roundabout and onto the road.

When you have completely left the roundabout, only then should you cancel your left-turn signal.

Things to know about roundabouts

Most importantly do not attach any time limit to emerge from a roundabout or road junction. Wait until there is a safe gap and time to move off safely and under full control. A good safety guide to help you to decide would be '*If in doubt – don't!*'

Another tip is to judge it as if you were a pedestrian. When would you walk across this road? If you would walk across the road, then it is safe to drive off. If you wouldn't begin to walk across, then it is not safe to drive off. Remember that you have been a pedestrian much longer than you have been a driver, so use your pedestrian experience. The speed that you could emerge onto the roundabout as a pedestrian is similar to the speed which you would move off in first gear in your car. It is only when you accelerate into second gear that your car is faster than if you were walking.

If you have waited for some time because of the heavy volume of traffic and then you take a chance and pull out causing another road-user to take avoiding action, not only would you fail your driving test, but more importantly, you are dangerous both to yourself and to other road-users. The fact that you have stopped to wait in itself suggests that you decided that it was not safe to proceed, so to pull out at a later time when it is still not safe, contradicts your initial assessment of the traffic situation. Basically: be patient and wait for a 'suitable' gap before pulling out.

> You can get a minor fault from your examiner for waiting too long, if by proceeding you wouldn't have caused the approaching vehicle to take any avoiding action, including having to reduce speed. But this would only be a minor point, unless you miss too may opportunities to move out. If you were to pull out and cause another driver to take evasive action, this would be a Serious or Dangerous fault resulting in a fail – or after your test, an accident.

Don't always assume that a driver coming towards you can see you. They might be distracted by something and not see you until it is too late. I always tell my pupils to imagine that the driver they are pulling in front of is sending a text message and is not concentrating. If you pull out in front of them in the hope that they will take evasive action, you might be in for a nasty surprise!

The drivers who have accidents are the people who wouldn't wait for a gap and just drove out hoping that the other cars would avoid them. As pedestrians, they would never have walked out in that same situation.

A lot of people get a little bit anxious with roundabouts, but actually, when you think about it, they are easier than crossroads for the simple reason that you only have to give way to traffic coming from your right. So as long as its clear on the right you should be able to proceed.

> If you should find that you have accidentally chosen the 'wrong' lane for where you were asked to go, or intended to go, abandon where you were going to go, and follow the direction for the lane that you are now in. You will NOT fail your driving test for going in the wrong direction. But you will fail your driving test if you attempt to change your course on the roundabout, particularly if you are forcing another road-user to take avoiding action.

If you are asked by your driving instructor or driving examiner to take the road leading straight ahead at the next roundabout, but you aren't sure which one they mean, the easiest way to decide which road is the one leading straight ahead is to think about the amount of turning the steering wheel will need. The road leading straight ahead is going to be the one which will need the least amount of turning.

When you approach a roundabout begin to plan 'an exit strategy' by looking for a landmark. For example: you are approaching a roundabout where you intend to take the third exit. Now look for a landmark such as a building, bus stop or road sign. As you enter the roundabout, you keep a lookout for your landmark, this will allow you to concentrate on your mirror, signal and position procedures instead of worrying about finding your exit.

When you approach a roundabout, visualise the roads off the roundabout the same as you would see a crossroads.

For example, at a crossroads, would you be confused which is the road to take you:

Left? Straight ahead? Right?

No, of course you wouldn't. So now when you put the roundabout 'circle' back into the centre of the crossroads it makes much more sense.

JUNCTIONS

Make sure that you've completed your MSM routine **before** you reach the junction, so that you're not finishing off the gear change and also trying to assess whether to proceed or not.

When waiting to turn at road junctions, don't spend more than about two seconds looking in any one direction. If you spend more time watching only in one direction, when it becomes clear, by the time you look in the opposite direction to weigh-up the traffic situation in this direction, you may well have missed your opportunity to emerge.

You need to treat your brain like a computer and keep it up to date with the very latest traffic data i.e. the current traffic situation in **both** directions.

Remember POM: prepare first, observe and only when you are sure it is safe, should you move off.

You are asked by your instructor or examiner to take the next turning on the left or right. The problem is, you can't see the junction. Then suddenly there it is, just a couple of car lengths in front of you! You have to rush your MSM routine and also safely negotiate the corner. Not exactly ideal.

When driving in urban areas you will see that most councils place street lights directly opposite road junctions. This is so that it lights up the junction at night to make it safer for all road users.

So when you are asked to take the next road junction on the left for example, you look out for any street lights on the right - which will be directly opposite the junction you're looking for. If it's not opposite the first street light, it will probably be opposite the next one. This gives you much more notice to carry out your MSM routine, safely and competently.

Give way

The 'GIVE WAY' sign is just the start of the sentence 'Give Way To Traffic On The Major Road'.

Approach Give Way junctions positively!

Because learners can lack confidence in their ability to control the car, they can also approach Give Way junctions quite negatively. In contrast, experienced drivers tend to approach Give Way junctions much more positively:

Learners tend to think *'I'm going to stop – unless it's clear'* while experienced drivers think *'I'm going to keep going – unless there's a problem'*.

Can you see the difference in outlook? It's not to say that you shouldn't slow down and assess the situation safely and accurately, but next time you are approaching a Give Way junction, ask yourself, do I need to come to a complete stop, or can I keep moving? Even if it means you may have to select first gear and 'crawl' forward.

Filter lanes

A 'filter lane' is a lane which is designed to take you to one side of the main road and allow the traffic behind to continue without needing to wait for you to complete your turn into a side road.

As you approach a side road which has a filter lane, after carrying out your MSM procedure, start looking out for the road markings. Avoid driving through any striped lines, as this is to separate you from the oncoming traffic. Be sure to not only get all four wheels into the filter lane, but position the car over to the right-hand side of it.

Normally you will see a double-headed arrow. One part of the arrow will be pointing straight ahead, the other will be pointing to the right towards the entry point of the filter lane at the place where you are to enter. A good tip is to straddle the angled arrow which is pointing right, into the filter lane. This way you will not be entering too early or heading into any oncoming traffic.

It is also of importance to enter either into the centre of the filter lane, or preferably to the right of the filter lane close to the white line on your right. This way you shorten the distance between where you have stopped and the side road you are entering.

You can compare this to a pedestrian situation: when about to cross the road from a pavement, would you stand well back from the kerb, or closer to the edge of the kerb? Most people would stand quite close to the kerb to reduce the time and distance it takes to cross the road.

Therefore, be careful not to enter or wait on the left-hand side of the filter lane, as you have further to cross, and also you risk obstructing or being hit by traffic passing on your left, particularly by larger vehicles such as lorries or buses.

Stop lines

When approaching a Stop line, concentrate on stopping. This means being aware of what is behind you, your speed and position on approach, and where you need to position the vehicle when you bring it to a full and complete stop.

A lot of people tend to treat Stop junctions exactly the same as Give Way junctions. But they are completely different: at a Stop junction you **have** to stop completely. At a Give Way junction you only need to stop if, by proceeding, you would cause another road-user to take avoiding or evasive action.

Many people slow down on approaching a Stop line, but just before stopping they see that the road is clear, and continue without bringing the car to a complete halt. They will say *'I did stop'* – even though they were still travelling at 2mph – or *'I was almost stopped'* or *'I was virtually stopped'*! Either you have stopped at the Stop line or you haven't!

If you approached a red traffic light, would you continue? Even if no-one else is on the road as you approach the red ones? No of course you wouldn't. Treat the Stop line just like a **red** traffic light. After you have stopped and decide that it is safe to proceed, then, and only then, you should treat the junction as a **green** traffic light.

ROAD MARKINGS AND SIGNS

Look at all road signs and road markings as your friends. They are there to help you to avoid getting into difficulties. Just like your real friends would. If your friends were familiar with the local area, they would be would be helping you out by saying things like *'you'd better slow down here, it's a really sharp bend'* or *'there's a railway level crossing coming up, so expect to see a queue of traffic'* or even *'there's a hump-back bridge coming up and you won't be able to see who is coming the other way until you're on top of the bridge'*.

Remember that when you're driving, **all** of the road signs and markings are a friend talking to **you**!

A good rule for understanding the different white lines in the middle of the road is: The more paint, the more danger. The less paint, the less danger.

The shortest white lines in the centre of the road generally mean that the road is hazard-free or minimal hazards. The longer white lines are Hazard Warning lines. These could be on approach to road junctions, brows of hills, road narrows, hump back bridges or bends. In other words, you need to be more careful, particularly when weighing up whether to overtake another vehicle. You should avoid crossing the continuous white line in the centre of the road, as these would normally be placed where visibility is severely restricted.

When you see the word Slow painted on the road, you should drive slower than the prevailing speed limit. For example if you are in a 40mph, drive less than 40mph, in a 30mph, drive less than 30mph.

If you see the word Slow painted on the road more than once, it's almost like they're saying it louder! So each successive time you see the word, you should reduce your speed even further. For example, in a 30mph, at the first word you may reduce to 25mph, the next one to 20mph, another one perhaps to 15mph, and so on.

OVERTAKING

When should you overtake?

You should only overtake if you can do so safely and legally, you can see that the way ahead is clear and that you have sufficient time to complete the manoeuvre before another vehicle approaches. You must make sure that your view will not be obstructed by a blind bend, or the brow of a hill, and that you can complete the manoeuvre within the speed limit. If you cannot overtake without exceeding the speed limit then the vehicle in front of you is not really holding you up. Make sure that the vehicle behind you is not beginning to overtake you.

You should not overtake where there are hatched road markings, at or near road junctions, or where there is a 'no overtaking' sign.

How do you overtake?

Before overtaking another moving vehicle you need to evaluate if you are sure the risk is worth the reward. What this means is that by overtaking, will you be making significant progress or will you be just one vehicle further ahead? If the latter, then it really isn't worth the risk.

Overtaking is one of the riskiest manoeuvres and should not be taken lightly.

Would you risk losing £10.00 to win just £10.50? And if you had the opportunity to overtake one vehicle, but there are another 20 vehicles ahead of them, and the road has quite a few bends and lots of oncoming traffic - would you do it?

Now, if you were going to bet £10.00 on a 'sure thing', but you have the chance to win £100.00, then this might be a much more sensible risk. Given the chance to overtake a slow moving tractor on a very straight and clear stretch of road, with no oncoming traffic and no vehicles ahead of the tractor, that might be worth the risk – but you would still want to make sure it was as sure a bet as possible.

A friend of mine was driving home to West Berkshire from his in-laws' in Kent. He and his wife were driving the journey of around 125 miles in separate cars. Now, at the time he had a new Peugeot 205 1.9 GTI and he used to drive it at high speed, often over the legal speed limits, tailgating the vehicle in front and flashing his lights to get them to move over. His wife drove a Peugeot 104, base model. She used to drive at a very average speed of around 40mph and very steadily.

That day, my friend got home and put the kettle on to make himself a cup of tea, feeling quite exhausted after his fast, furious and frantic drive home. Before the kettle finished boiling his wife arrived home. That's when he really realised that no matter how furiously you drive, when you catch up with the next road-user you'll still be having to bide your time until there is another opportunity to pass them. His wife drove slow and steady and the difference was less than the time that the kettle took to boil. But who took the most risks? And for the reward of being home just a couple of minutes before the safe driver.

Will it really make a difference to pass the vehicle in front? Is it really worth the risk? Is the reward greater than the risk?

Overtaking on a dual carriageway

Begin by signalling to the right to inform the following and surrounding traffic of your intention.

Now I don't mean signal and go! But, signal to 'ask'. You're not 'telling' people what you are going to do, you're asking and then observing the reaction to your signal **before** you make a decision to make your move, or not.

Your signal does **not** give you the right to make your move. But you do need to give a signal when you know that a lane change is imminent. Be careful not to wait until it is clear before giving your signal, because if you don't signal, no one will know what your intention is and therefore are given the option to help you out.

I've often been overtaking vehicles on a motorway or dual-carriageway and as I am going past I observe the driver checking their right-hand side mirror deciding when to give their signal. If they had signalled when they first thought of changing lanes, I may well have let them out in front of me if the traffic conditions permitted.

Please note: you need your indicator to flash at least 3 times **before** carrying out your manoeuvre to allow other road users to be aware of your intentions, before you change your road position.

Overtaking cyclists

You should only overtake the cyclist at the first **safe** opportunity. So **not** just the first opportunity, you need to make sure that it is safe for all road users. Treat them much like a parked car. If it's a straight, clear piece of road, and there is nothing immediately approaching you, you should check both your interior centre mirror and right-hand door mirror and, if it is safe to overtake, move out giving as much room as possible. This will allow for the cyclist to be avoiding a drain cover, pothole or some other uneven road surface.

A lot of learner drivers say that they don't like coming across cyclists when they are driving, but they then proceed to follow them for much longer than absolutely necessary. Imagine if you were at a party, would you stand next to the person you least like at that party? Or would you try to get away from them at the first available safe opportunity?

Overtaking horses

The very first thing to do is check your mirrors and slow down to assess the situation. Don't follow too closely. You should only overtake when it is safe for everyone.

Your top priority is not to frighten or spook the horse. If you do, the horse may well rear up or leap into the road causing a danger to the rider, itself and other road-users. Whatever you do, do not sound your horn or shout at the rider or horse as you pass by. Look at the situation from a purely selfish point of view: if you frighten the horse, it may end up kicking or bumping into your car, or throwing the rider off onto or in front of your car.

If the horse looks very agitated, or the rider is having problems keeping it under control, wait until the rider beckons you through. The rider knows their own horse better than you do.

When passing the horse and rider, give a wide berth and keep as far away from them as possible. Drive slowly past, but not too slowly, as the horse will be aware that you are there and if you are too slow, the horse may well get agitated wondering where you are, or whether you pose a danger or threat to them.

DRIVING PAST PARKED CARS AND OBSTRUCTIONS

When passing parked cars, it is very easy to end up just missing them. In fact, you give just enough distance to get past without bumping it. But ideally you want to give at least a door's width. This is just in case the car door should open, or the car should move off. The way I like to explain it, is that if they open the door and you feel the need to swerve, wherever you swerve to is where you should have been. Put yourself in that position to start with.

When people are going past parked cars, they tend to slow down because they're worried that a car is going to come the other way. Imagine you're teaching me to cross the road. We both stand on the pavement, we look up and down the road: it's clear. We walk across the road, you get to the pavement and you turn around and I'm still halfway across the road and you say 'what are you doing?' and I say 'a car might come!' So obviously if a car might come I'd be better off on the opposite pavement as soon as possible.

In other words, when you're walking on the pavement, you don't then walk slower across the road than you'd been walking on the pavement. If you'd been strolling on the pavement you're going to walk a little bit quicker across the road, and then stroll again when you get to the pavement. When you overtake a parked or stalled car, you're on the wrong side of the road, and you want to be on the wrong side of the road for the least amount of time.

So rather than slow down when you go past that car, if the road is clear and straight and you can see it's clear to overtake, you need to do a little burst of speed, just accelerate a little bit, to get past that car, and when you come back to your side of the road you can slow down to your normal speed.

My driving instructor used to say to me: if you're going to have an accident then have it on your side of the road, because then you can blame the other guy. But if you're on their side of the road then it makes it difficult actually pin the blame on them. The best you've got is 'Didn't you see me coming?'

If you can't give this amount of clearance, you should consider stopping and giving way to any oncoming vehicle.

When meeting an oncoming vehicle driving down a road with parked vehicles on both sides, you don't need to decide whether you should go first or to give way to the oncoming vehicle. Just do the opposite to what the oncoming vehicle does. If the oncoming vehicle stops, you should proceed. If the oncoming vehicle proceeds, you should stop.

There is no point in you both coming to a stop or you both proceeding.

This way you don't have to worry what to do if you should come across this situation, you just react to the actions of the other motorist. Liken this to a pedestrian situation. You don't worry what if, when you go out of your front door, you meet another pedestrian approaching in the opposite direction, you tend to just pass them on the opposite side, or let their behaviour guide you.

ANTICIPATING THE ROAD AHEAD AND BEING AWARE OF POTENTIAL HAZARDS

There are lots of factors that can affect your driving: bad weather, different types of roads, road surface and congestion.

When you're driving, you need to watch and plan and anticipate as far ahead as you can. Be careful not to just be looking at the end of your car, not even the car in front, you want to be looking as far as you can, maybe at the furthest vehicle, maybe at the next set of traffic lights, the next roundabout, the next road junction coming up. If you can see what's going on ahead of you, you can prepare and not get caught out.

So rather than wait until the cars ahead slow down, you can slow down sooner. A lot of people tend to just watch the car in front, so when that car suddenly stops they end up very close, or even bump into the back of that car. If they had lifted their gaze, looked much further ahead, they might not have been caught out.

I always tell my pupils: *'I'm five steps ahead of you, because I'm watching what's going on. I'm giving you the chance to see what's going on, giving you the chance to react to it and if you don't, I'm ready to jump in and help you.'* All driving instructors are doing this. We wouldn't last 5 minutes of any driving lesson if we didn't! But what driving instructors should be doing - and most of them are – is teaching you to drive and make the decisions that they would also make in that same situation. The key is, the further ahead you look, the fewer emergencies are going to arise.

Observation

Drive as though you have a 100 metre bubble all around your car.

Observe everything which is happening within that bubble, to the left, to the right, behind as well as in front of you, and frequently check these areas. If you know precisely what is happening at all times within your 100 metre bubble, you are less likely to get involved in any accident threatening incidents.

Not only are you observing vehicles, road layout changes, traffic signs, traffic lights and lane markings, but also the drivers around you and what they are doing.

When the driver behind you is no longer following you, you will have a new driver to assess, so you need to be aware of the driving style of the new driver. At the same time, you need to be aware of where you are going, making sure that you're in the correct lane or road position, that you are observing the road signs and traffic lights, that you are driving at an appropriate and legal speed limit and that you are in the correct gear and fully concentrated on driving your vehicle safely and under your control at all times.

When driving along take notice and be observant. The obvious is very easy to overlook.

For example. if you notice a bus stop, then you're on a bus route. If you notice people standing at the bus stop on the right-hand side of the road, then the bus is due. This way you won't be surprised or caught out, particularly if you are driving in a narrow road or a road congested with parked cars.

When you see vans, pick-up trucks parked at the side of the road during the daytime, expect to see workmen and activity around the vans, particularly as they create 'blind spots' because of their lack of side windows to observe other potential hazards. In the evenings they are generally parked up where the owner lives, but still watch out for parked cars and driveways hidden by those vans and pick-up trucks.

When you see vehicle doors or car boots open, start looking out for children and dogs. Be ready to slow down and/or stop.

Another example would be to notice than rubbish bins are out. This means that it is probably bin day on this particular road. So now you are looking out for the bin lorry. How can you tell if the bin lorry has already been? Apart from the obvious of bin lids not fully closed because, look at the bin handles. If the bin handles are facing into the road, the bin lorry hasn't been yet, as the householders tend to pull the bin out from their property and leave it ready for the bin men to empty. But when the bin men have been, they tend to pull the bin back towards the property so that the handle is now facing the property. Again, this is very easy observation to overlook, but can be very useful for your anticipation of meeting the bin lorry in a narrow or congested road.

> When approaching a sharp bend, try to look around the corner by looking for the straight part of the road. You will find that you naturally adjust your speed and steering without being conscious of doing so.

Oncoming traffic

When meeting oncoming traffic, particularly larger vehicles in small roads, check whether the wheels of the oncoming vehicle are on their own side of the centre line. It is very easy to feel intimidated by the presence of an oncoming vehicle, particularly a larger lorry or bus, but you can reassure yourself that it is safe to continue if you see that their wheels are on their own side of the road.

DUAL CARRIAGEWAYS AND MOTORWAYS

A dual carriageway is defined as a road in which the traffic from the opposite direction has been separated from you by a central reservation. This means there are two separate strips of tarmac for roads travelling in opposite directions, with a raised barrier between the two. This barrier can be grass, concrete or metal, but will mean that it would not be possible to roll a ball from one side of the road to the other.

The national speed limit on a dual carriageway is currently a maximum of 70mph, which is the same as a motorway. Speed limits may vary in certain places, as on all roads.

Dual carriageways can often have side roads and lay-bys that lead onto single carriageways, and there can also be cross-roads where joining traffic will cross over from one side to the other. They will normally have a central reservation where the crossing traffic can cross in two stages. All types of vehicles can use dual carriageways including cyclists, mopeds and tractors, even mobility scooters and pedestrians.

Dual carriageways have an advantage over normal two-way roads as they provide the opportunity to overtake slower moving vehicles safely, removing the potential hazard of any approaching traffic.

You do need to be extra careful when about to overtake on a dual carriageway, because of the potential of encountering faster traffic approaching from behind you in the right-hand lane. Some vehicles will be travelling much faster than you realise, and could possibly be exceeding the speed limit. Don't rely on the vehicle approaching from behind to slow down or allow you enter the lane in front of them.

Slip road

A 'slip road' is either an acceleration lane or a deceleration lane depending on whether you are joining or leaving a dual carriageway or motorway. When joining a dual carriageway or motorway, the slip is there to ensure that you can build up your speed in attempt to match the speed of the vehicles that are already on the carriageway, and to minimise the difference between your speed and theirs.

Motorway slip roads, by law, have to be a minimum of a quarter of a mile, so it's a lot easier to adjust your speed by increasing or reducing it in order to find a safe gap to join the traffic on the main carriageway.

Joining dual-carriageways and motorways

When attempting to join via the slip road, lookout for a large or slow vehicle in the left-hand lane. Very often there is a 'vacuum' behind the slower vehicle, as the traffic approaching it has already moved to the lane to the right of that vehicle. This could be your opportunity to join safely.

Be especially careful when there are several large or slow vehicles, as you will normally want to feed in behind the last one, unless there is a safe gap between them, where you won't end up too close to the one ahead and that you will have no effect on the one you join in front of.

When joining a dual-carriageway with a short slip road, your intention is to join safely and to attempt to match the speed of the traffic already on the dual-carriageway. You should do so without causing that traffic to take any avoiding action. Remember that as you join there is a broken white Give Way line between the slip road and the main carriageway. Be prepared as you would at any other Give Way line to slow down or stop if necessary.

Be extra careful when building up speed to make sure that you have not only checked your rear view and right-hand side door mirror, but also performed at least one check of your blindspot over your right shoulder. If necessary be prepared to stop, but also be aware of any following vehicles also on the slip road behind you.

Many road-users think that they are not allowed to stop on a slip-road. Of course you are allowed to stop to avoid causing another road-user taking evasive action, but your intention is to increase your speed and join if it is safe to do so. Therefore, your intention should be to build up speed in the filter lane, aiming to match the speed of the traffic already on the carriageway, but ready to slow down or stop if necessary.

Remember, that unless you're driving a powerful, large-engine car, your car will stop more quickly than it can build up speed. So your priority is to build up speed initially, but be ready to slow down or stop if necessary, to avoid causing any problem to others already on the dual-carriageway.

When driving on a motorway or dual-carriageway you will occasionally come across a temporary limited speed sign such as a 50mph speed limit instead of 70mph speed limit. With modern cars it can be difficult to keep your speed limit to 50mph after driving at 70mph for quite some time, and can be distracting whilst constantly checking that you're not exceeding the speed limit.

The easiest way to overcome this is to keep to the left lane where you will find those vehicles which are normally obeying the temporary speed limit. This way you do not need to constantly keep checking your speed limit but instead you can be observing the traffic and being alert for any potential hazards.

Leaving a motorway or dual carriageway

Leaving a dual carriageway is a little easier. There will be a destination road sign half a mile before the next exit. Ideally, make sure that you are in the left-hand lane before you reach this sign, to ensure that you don't miss your exit, or cause other vehicles in the left lane to take evasive action as you move to the left lane.

As you approach the 300 yard marker sign, which is a sign with three sloped white lines, signal your intention to take the exit lane to the left. Wait until you reach and enter the deceleration slip road before reducing too much speed, whilst being aware of any traffic following you onto the slip road. After driving at high speed for quite some time, 40mph can easily feel like 20mph, so watch your speedometer as you reach the end of your slip road.

MANOEUVRES

As of December 2017, the four manoeuvres that you might be asked to perform consist of:

Reversing into a parking bay

Driving forwards into a bay, and reversing out

Parallel parking

Pull up on the right and reverse

PLAN A – to get your manoeuvre done correctly on the 1st attempt

PLAN B – do whatever is necessary to complete the manoeuvre

PLAN C – don't give up on the manoeuvre

All of these manoeuvres should be carried out slowly by using very strict 'clutch control'. On all of the manoeuvres carried out on the driving test you will be judged on two things, your control and your observation.

Whilst carrying out most of the test manoeuvres, keeping the 'gas' set just ensures that the engine does not stall – therefore the 'gas' does **not** control the speed of the vehicle at this time. The clutch, however, **does** control the speed of the vehicle. The higher the clutch is allowed to come up, the faster the vehicle will move. The lower the clutch is put down, the slower the vehicle will move. The point at where the vehicle engine note just begins to fade, and the car is about to move, is commonly referred to as the 'bite' point. By using the bite point you will be able to inch your vehicle backwards or forwards ensuring complete control over the speed that you allow your vehicle to move.

To practice any of these manoeuvres, select a quiet area, ensuring that you choose a safe and convenient place to stop your car. Do not start the exercise until you are sure that it is clear and safe to begin to move, and that you will not endanger or inconvenience any other road-users, including pedestrians. If any other road-users are present, you need to wait to ensure that it is safe to begin the manoeuvre and if in doubt, wait until you are convinced that it is safe to proceed.

Remember that no matter in which direction you are moving your vehicle, forwards or backwards, you must wait if any pedestrians or cyclists are passing your vehicle. This is to ensure complete safety, in case your foot inadvertently slipped off one of the pedals for example.

The examiner could use a wide variety of car parks for the bay parking exercise, such as hotels, retail parks and supermarkets. They will use suitable car parks depending on each test centre. You don't need to park in a bay where there are other vehicles beside you.

The examiner will ask you to park in a bay, either driving forwards into the bay and reversing out, or reversing in and driving out forwards. The examiner will tell you which one they want you to do.

You can't drive through a first parking bay, and then park in a bay directly in front of that one. When you reverse out, you can't go into any bays behind you.

Reversing into a parking bay

'I'd like you to reverse into a convenient parking bay finishing within the lines, either to the left or the right'

Once you have chosen the parking bay you intend to park in, pull up and stop about 1 to 1.5 metres out from the end of the parking bay box and about two car lengths forward of the parking bay. Decide if you need to signal to any other road-users as you stop. Put the handbrake on and select neutral.

At this point it would be a good idea to adjust your side mirrors downwards so that you can see the wheel arches and the lines showing the edges of the parking bay.

Remember POM POM. Prepare, Observe, Manoeuvre. Select reverse gear ready to move backwards, as when you select reverse gear it automatically switches on the white reversing lights on the back of your car.

Take a good look all round the car, being aware of any other road-users such as vehicles, pedestrians or cyclists nearby, and wait if necessary or if in doubt. As soon as it is clear to do so, move the car very slowly backwards under strict clutch control, when you 'feel' that you are about a bay and half away from your target location, begin turning the steering wheel to the right.

Keep checking all round your car for any passing traffic, pedestrians and cyclists, by looking out of ALL of the windows, including turning around and looking through the rear window, as well as checking all three mirrors (interior rear view, and both side mirrors). Allow the car to enter the parking bay under very strict clutch control. As the car becomes straight, straighten up the steering wheel as well as checking both side mirrors to ensure that you are in the centre of the bay. Make any necessary adjustments to the steering wheel.

Watch through the back window to ensure that you do not go too far back and into another vehicle or other obstruction.

Try to have an equal amount of space on either side of the car. If necessary, be prepared to pull your car forward, completely out of the parking bay with all four wheels. Checking your side mirrors, turn the steering wheel towards the wider gap, until it looks even, then straighten the steering wheel.

Keep checking all round your car for passing traffic, pedestrians and cyclists, by looking out of ALL of the windows and checking all three mirrors.

Stop the car. Handbrake on. Select neutral.

'Now, I'd like you to drive forwards out, to the (left/right).'

Remember POM POM. Prepare, Observe, Manoeuvre. Select first gear and be ready to move forwards. As soon as it is clear to do so, aim to move the front of your car very slowly under very strict clutch control, and keeping the steering wheel straight. When you 'feel' that you are half way out of the bay, or your shoulder is in line or just past the end of the parking bay, begin turning the steering wheel either to the left or to the right whichever way you have chosen to go.

STEP 1

Pull up and stop about a metre to a metre and a half out from the end of the parking bay box and about two car lengths forward of the parking bay. As soon as it is clear to move, move the car very slowly backwards under strict clutch control

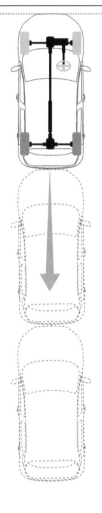

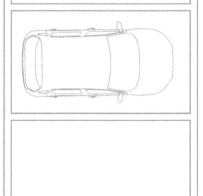

Target parking bay

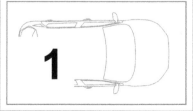

STEP 2

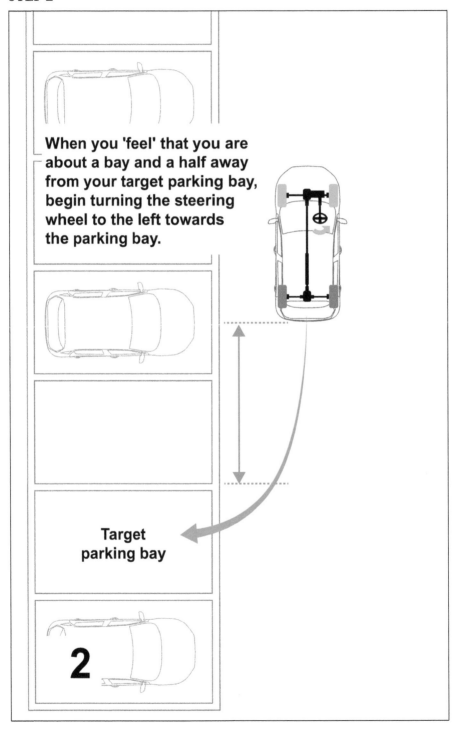

When you 'feel' that you are about a bay and a half away from your target parking bay, begin turning the steering wheel to the left towards the parking bay.

Target parking bay

STEP 3

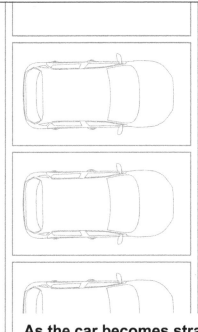

As the car becomes straight,
straighten up the steering wheel
as well as checking both
side mirrors to ensure that you
are in the centre of the bay.
Make any necessary adjustments
to the steering wheel.

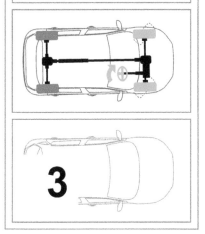

3

STEP 4

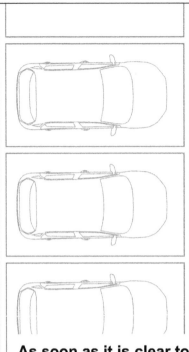

As soon as it is clear to do so, aim to move the front of your car very slowly under very strict clutch control, and keeping the steering wheel straight.

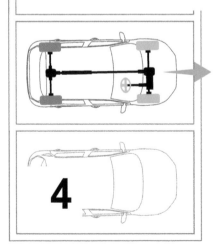

STEP 5

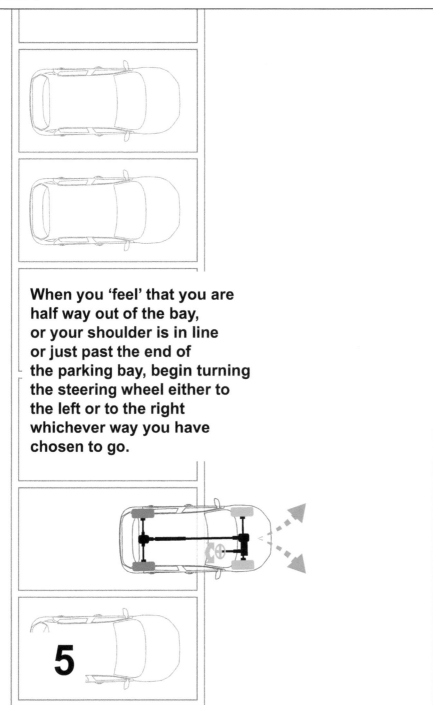

When you 'feel' that you are
half way out of the bay,
or your shoulder is in line
or just past the end of
the parking bay, begin turning
the steering wheel either to
the left or to the right
whichever way you have
chosen to go.

Driving forwards into a bay, and reversing out

"I'd like you to drive forward into a convenient parking bay finishing within the lines, either to the left or the right"

Remember POM POM. Prepare, Observe, Manoeuvre. Select first gear and be ready to move forwards.

Position your car between 1.5 and 2 metres out from your target parking bay. Take a good look all round the car, being aware of any other road-users such as vehicles, pedestrians or cyclists nearby. Wait if necessary or if in doubt.

As soon as it is clear to do so, under very strict clutch control, aim to move the front of your car very slowly into the far left (if the bay is to your right) or far right (if the bay is to your left) of the beginning of your chosen parking bay.

When you 'feel' that you are very close to the front of the bay, and the car becomes straight, begin turning the steering wheel quickly to the opposite direction to straighten up, checking both side mirrors to ensure that you have all four wheels between the parking bay lines. Make any necessary adjustments to the steering wheel.

Keep checking all round your car for passing traffic and pedestrians and cyclists, by looking out of the windows and checking all three mirrors.

As you drive forward into the bay, you may find it difficult to judge how much room that you have in front of your car and when to stop. To help you to judge this, your right foot which is on the gas pedal is just over the front wheel arch. So your right foot is just behind the front wheel. As you get further into the bay, look out of your front driver's side window to see where the kerb is and in relation to where your right foot is as this will help you to more accurately judge when to stop your car.

If necessary, be prepared to reverse back out, looking all around your car as you do so for any other road users, and enter again while readjusting your steering to ensure that you finish with all four wheels between the bay lines.

Stop the car. Handbrake on and Select neutral.

Once you have finished the examiner will say:

'Now, I'd like you to reverse out to the (left/right).'

Remember POM POM. Prepare, Observe, Manoeuvre. Select reverse gear ready to move backwards.

Take a good look all round the car being aware of any other road-users such as vehicles, pedestrians or cyclists nearby, and wait if necessary or if in doubt.

As soon as it is clear to do so, reverse very slowly under very strict clutch control, and keeping the steering wheel straight. When you 'feel' that you are half way out of the bay, or your shoulder is in line or just past the end of the parking bay, begin turning the steering wheel either to the left or to the right, whichever way you have chosen to go.

As you are reversing, keep continually checking every few seconds all round your car for passing traffic and pedestrians and cyclists, by looking out of all of the windows and checking all three mirrors (interior rear view, and both side mirrors).

Stop the car. Handbrake on and select neutral.

STEP 1

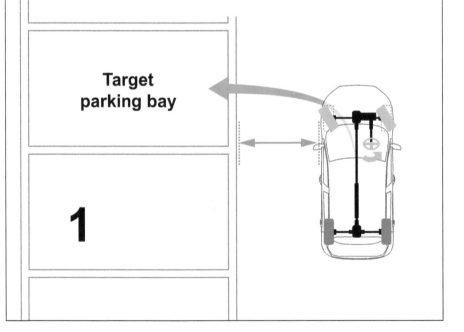

Position your car between 1.5 and 2 metres out from your target parking bay. As soon as it is clear to do so, aim to move the front of your car very slowly into the far left (if the bay is to your right) or far right (if the bay is to your left) of the beginning of your chosen parking bay.

Target parking bay

1

STEP 2

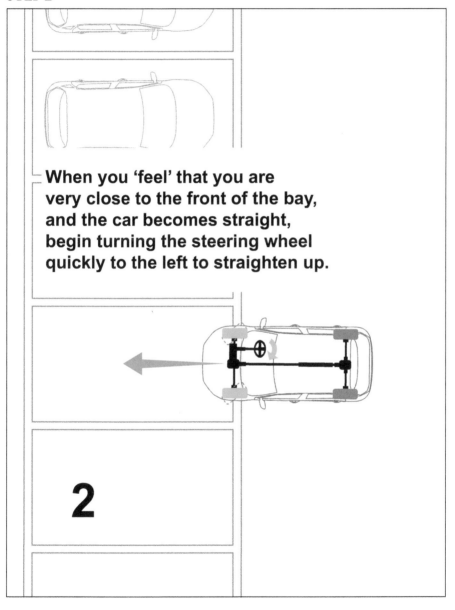

When you 'feel' that you are
very close to the front of the bay,
and the car becomes straight,
begin turning the steering wheel
quickly to the left to straighten up.

2

STEP 3

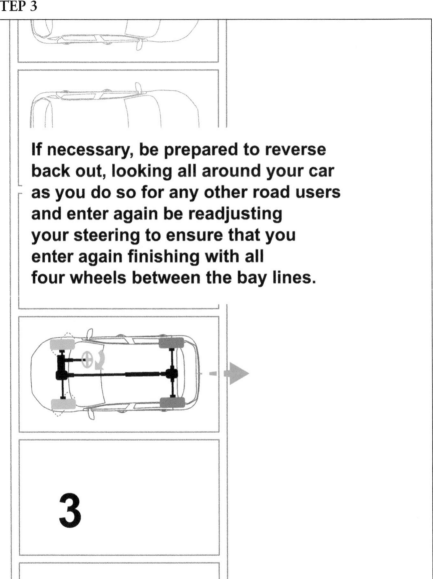

If necessary, be prepared to reverse
back out, looking all around your car
as you do so for any other road users
and enter again be readjusting
your steering to ensure that you
enter again finishing with all
four wheels between the bay lines.

3

STEP 4

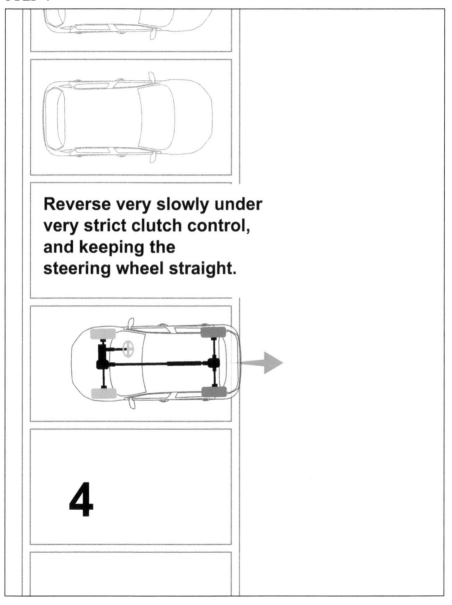

Reverse very slowly under very strict clutch control, and keeping the steering wheel straight.

4

STEP 5

When you 'feel' that you are
half way out of the bay,
or your shoulder is in line
or just past the end of
the parking bay, begin turning
the steering wheel either to
the left or to the right
whichever way you have
chosen to go.

5

Parallel parking

'I would now like you to demonstrate the Parallel Park exercise. Pull up alongside the vehicle in front of us. Reverse back keeping reasonably close to the kerb, stop your car within two car lengths and parallel to the kerb. Move off when you are ready.'

For this manoeuvre, all you've got to do is focus on getting the rear wheel next to the kerb but not allow it to run into the kerb. Of course you need to do all round observations and watch out for any traffic – but just focus on getting the rear wheel next to the kerb and this way it doesn't matter whether it's a car you're reversing around, a van, a skip or even a big pile of rubbish.

To begin the exercise, select a quiet side road ensuring that you choose a safe and convenient place to stop next to the kerb. Ensure that you don't block or obstruct any entrances or driveways and that you don't stop opposite another vehicle or obstruction.

You should stop your vehicle on the left-hand side of the road about 2 or 3 car lengths before the vehicle you are intending to parallel park behind. Decide if you need to signal to any other road users as you stop. Handbrake on and select neutral.

At this point it would be a good idea to adjust your left-hand side door mirror downwards so that you can see the left rear wheel arch and the left hand kerb.

Some instructors will suggest you use other vehicles as reference points. But if you line up your door mirror with the back door handle of the car you're reversing around, if it's two door car it won't work or a van it won't work. Some will tell you at a certain point to turn the steering to full lock and when you reach an angle of 40 degrees to turn the wheel away from the kerb. But this gets very complicated and difficult to remember. Instead, just focus on where that rear wheel is, don't allow it to go into the kerb and you'll end up parked.

Remember POM POM. Prepare, Observe, Manoeuvre. Select 1st gear ready to move off.

Take a good look all round the car being aware of any other road users such as vehicles, pedestrians or cyclists nearby, and wait if necessary or in doubt.

As soon as it is clear and safe to move off, drive the car forwards very slowly, under strict clutch control, turning the steering wheel to the right. Aim to pull up alongside the target vehicle keeping a door width away and side by side. Stop your car. Handbrake on. Select neutral.

Select reverse gear. Find the clutch 'bite' point to take into account any camber of the road and to ensure that your car will not roll forward. Take all the time you need to be certain that you have the 'bite' point as the accuracy is much more important than the speed at which you get the car ready to move off.

Put your hand on the handbrake 'ready' to release it – but DON'T release it yet.

Remember to concentrate on POM POM. Prepare, Observe, Manoeuvre very slowly under strict clutch control.

Once you have the 'bite' point, you are now ready for the 'O' of POM POM, Observation. Look out of every window of your car to make sure that the road is absolutely clear. If anyone is approaching, wait to see what they do next. If they wait for you, you should continue. If they continue, you should wait. So effectively you don't need to make the decision. 'they' make it for you, and you just do the opposite to what 'they' do,

When you are satisfied that it is safe to proceed, you have reached the 'M' for Manoeuvre part of the exercise. Release the handbrake and watch over your left shoulder maintaining strict clutch control to keep your car moving very slowly backwards. Keep a constant lookout for approaching road users from in front and behind.

When you 'feel' that your rear bumper has just passed the back of your target vehicle, turn the steering wheel 'towards' the kerb, whilst maintain strict clutch control. If necessary, because of the camber of the road, you may need to use the footbrake to control the speed of your car.

Now watch the left-hand door mirror. When you 'feel' that the rear wheel – nearest the kerb – is getting closer to the kerb, turn the steering wheel gently and gradually 'away' from the kerb.

Keep a constant lookout for approaching road users from in front and behind. When you 'feel' that your car is straight and parallel with the kerb, turn the steering 'towards' from the kerb to 'straighten up'. Stop the car. Handbrake on. Select neutral.

If necessary, move the car forwards again, but remember to allow yourself enough room to move off after you have completed the manoeuvre.

STEP 1

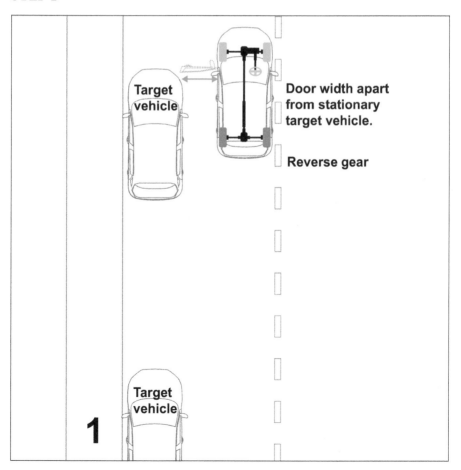

STEP 2

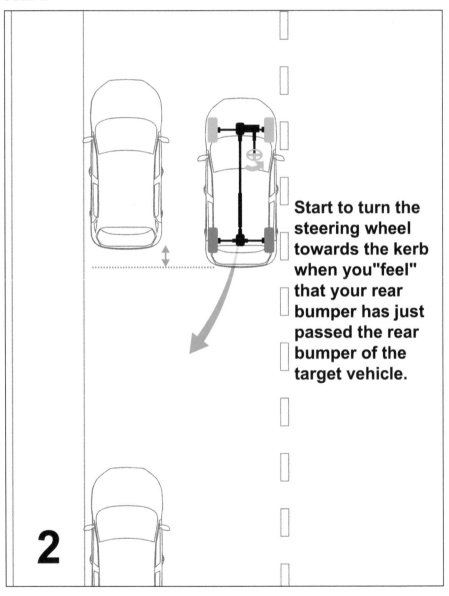

Start to turn the steering wheel towards the kerb when you"feel" that your rear bumper has just passed the rear bumper of the target vehicle.

2

STEP 3

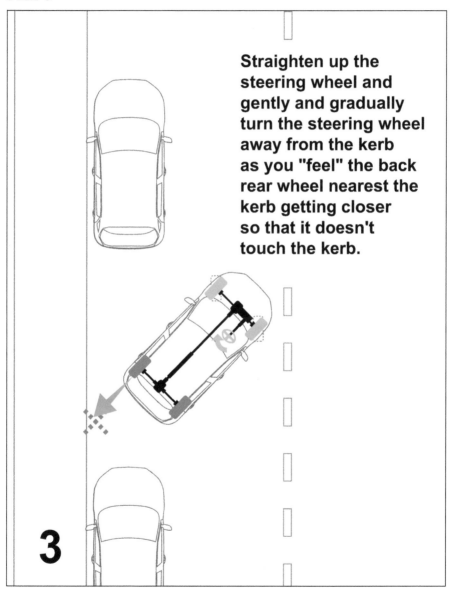

Straighten up the
steering wheel and
gently and gradually
turn the steering wheel
away from the kerb
as you "feel" the back
rear wheel nearest the
kerb getting closer
so that it doesn't
touch the kerb.

3

STEP 4

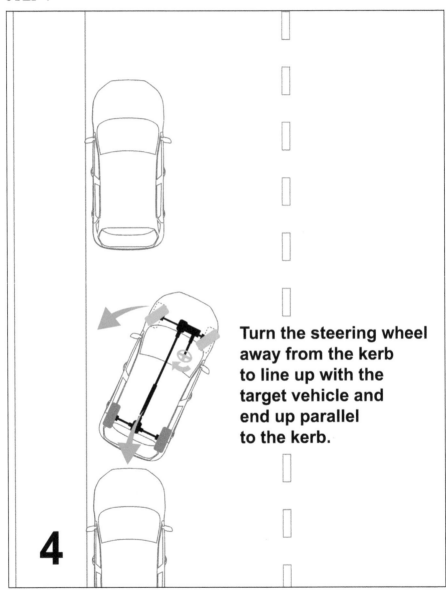

Turn the steering wheel
away from the kerb
to line up with the
target vehicle and
end up parallel
to the kerb.

4

STEP 5

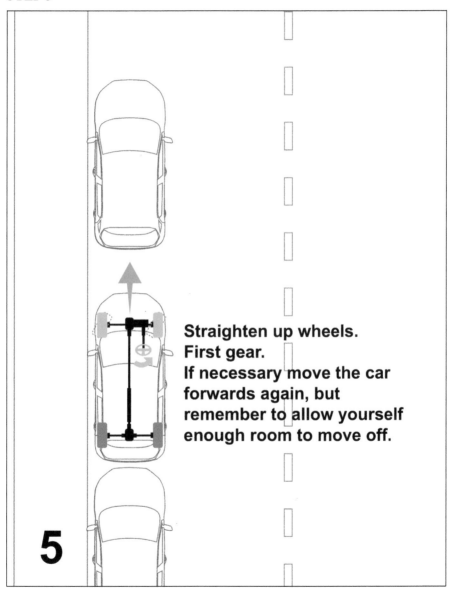

Straighten up wheels.
First gear.
If necessary move the car forwards again, but remember to allow yourself enough room to move off.

5

Pull up on the right and reverse

'Pull up on the right when it is safe to so, please.'

The full manoeuvre asked for here is to pull over from the left-hand side to the right, park on the right-hand side of the road, reverse back two car lengths and then drive back across to the left-hand side of the road

The examiner will give you the instruction while you're driving: they won't pull over first to give the instruction.

Remember POM POM. Prepare, Observe, Manoeuvre. Look for a safe and convenient place on the right-hand side of the road and, once you've found a suitable place, check your rear-view mirror, signal to the right, check your side mirror and watch for any approaching traffic, and wait if necessary for a safe gap in the traffic to cross the road. Once you reach the right-hand side of the road, pull forwards to ensure that both the front and rear of your car are straight and parallel with the kerb. Stop the car. Handbrake on, and select neutral.

'I'd now like you to reverse back for about two car lengths, keeping reasonably close to the kerb.'

Select reverse gear, set the gas and have your hand on the handbrake ready to release. Check all around your car, continue to keep looking around including through the back window, not just the rear view mirror, if any road user approaches stop before they pass your car. Reverse back two car lengths using strict clutch control, keeping the car straight and reasonably close to the right-hand kerb. After two car lengths, stop your car, put the handbrake on and select neutral.

WHEN YOU ARE READY TO DRIVE ON

Prepare by selecting first gear, setting the gas, with your hand on the handbrake ready to release. Check all your mirrors, check ahead, check your blind spot over your **left** shoulder as this will be where the rear approaching traffic will come from. Signal to the left, keep observing to the front and over your left shoulder and left side mirror as you move across to the left-hand side of the road again. Once you have reached the left-hand side of the road, safely begin to build up speed to match the speed of the other traffic.

STEP 1

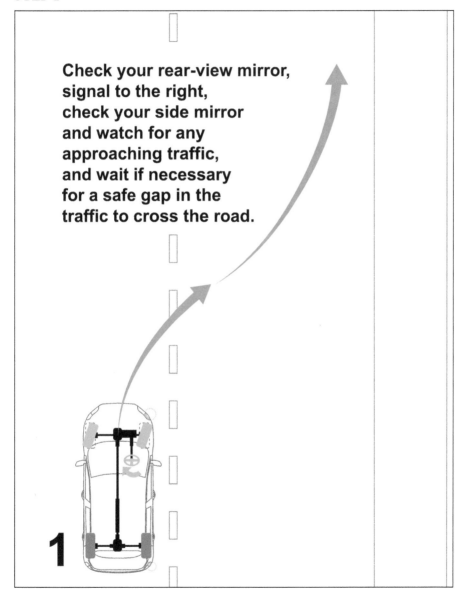

Check your rear-view mirror,
signal to the right,
check your side mirror
and watch for any
approaching traffic,
and wait if necessary
for a safe gap in the
traffic to cross the road.

STEP 2

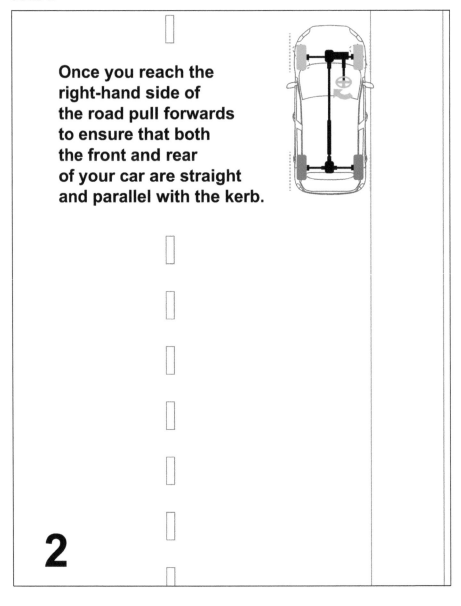

**Once you reach the
right-hand side of
the road pull forwards
to ensure that both
the front and rear
of your car are straight
and parallel with the kerb.**

2

STEP 3

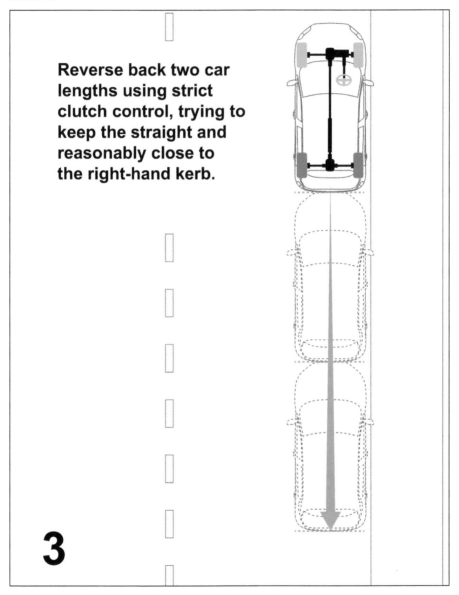

Reverse back two car lengths using strict clutch control, trying to keep the straight and reasonably close to the right-hand kerb.

3

STEP 4

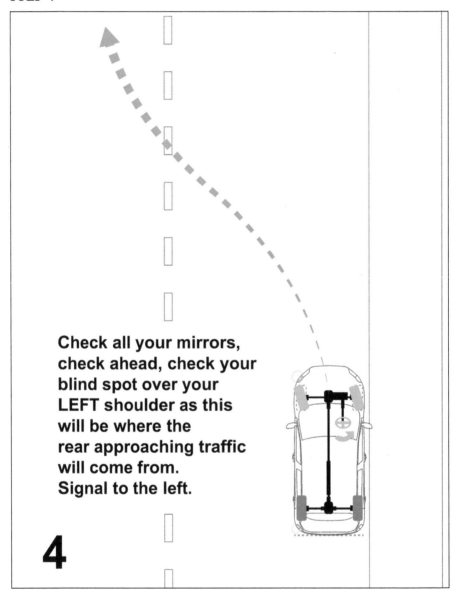

Check all your mirrors, check ahead, check your blind spot over your LEFT shoulder as this will be where the rear approaching traffic will come from. Signal to the left.

4

STEP 5

Keep observing to the front and over your left shoulder and left side mirror as you move across to the left-hand side of the road again.

5

Turn in the Road
no longer requested in the practical test

Although the turn in the road is no longer asked for in your driving test, it is still a very useful manoeuvre to learn, as it helps with clutch and steering control at low speed. This is particularly useful if you are going to reverse or drive onto or out of a narrow driveway, or if you need to drive out of a narrow space between vehicles.

Pull up and stop at the side of the at a safe and convenient place. Decide if you need to signal to any other road-users as you stop. Handbrake on. Select neutral.

Remember POM POM. Prepare, Observe, Manoeuvre. Select 1st gear ready to move off.

Take a good look out of all of the windows of the car being aware of any other road-users such as vehicles, pedestrians or cyclists nearby, and wait if necessary or if in doubt.

As soon as it is clear to move off, move the car very slowly under strict clutch control, turning the steering wheel quickly and fully to the right.

When you are nearly at the kerb, while keeping the car moving very slowly, quickly turn the wheel to the left to straighten up the wheels. Stop the car. Handbrake on. Select Neutral.

Now remember, at this point, not to distracted by anyone waiting, but to concentrate on POM POM. The first part being Preparation.

Select reverse gear. Find the clutch 'bite' point to take into account the camber of the road and to ensure that the car will not roll forward. Take all the time you need to be certain that you have got the 'bite' point, as the accuracy is much more important than the speed.

Put your hand on the handbrake 'ready' to release it – but DON'T release it yet.

Once you have the 'bite' point, you are now ready for the O of POM POM, Observation. Look out of every window in the car to make sure that the road is absolutely clear. If anyone is approaching, wait to see what they do next. If they wait for you, you should continue. If they continue, you should wait.

When you are satisfied that it is safe to proceed, you have reached the M for Manoeuvre part of the exercise. Release the handbrake and watch over your left shoulder, maintaining strict clutch control to keep the car moving very slowly back, turning the steering wheel quickly and fully to the left. Once you reach full-lock where the steering wheel will not turn any further, this is your cue to look over your right shoulder to decide when to straighten the steering wheel by turning it quickly to the right, and to decide when to stop the car before reaching the kerb.

Stop the car. Handbrake on. Select neutral. Remember POM POM. Prepare, Observe, Manoeuvre. Select first gear ready to move off.

Find the clutch 'bite' point to take into account the camber of the road and put your hand on the handbrake 'ready' to release it – but DON'T release it yet.

Once you have the 'bite' point, look out of every window in the car to make sure that the road is absolutely clear. If anyone is approaching, wait to see what they do next.

Take a good look out of all of the windows of the car. As soon as it is clear to move off, move the car very slowly under strict clutch control, turning the steering wheel quickly and fully to the right.

As you complete the turn, check the rear view mirror and either continue along the road, or, if you intend to pull up to stop at the side of the road, check your mirror and decide if you need to give a signal and if necessary do so, and pull up and stop safely beside the kerb at a safe and convenient place.

STEP 1

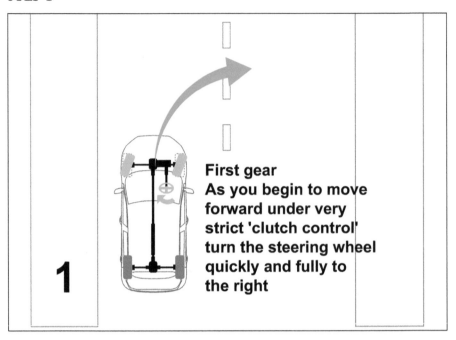

First gear
As you begin to move
forward under very
strict 'clutch control'
turn the steering wheel
quickly and fully to
the right

STEP 2

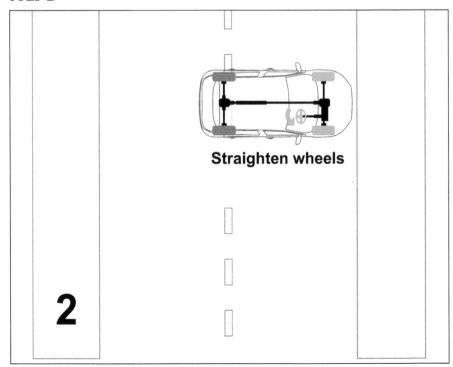

Straighten wheels

STEP 3

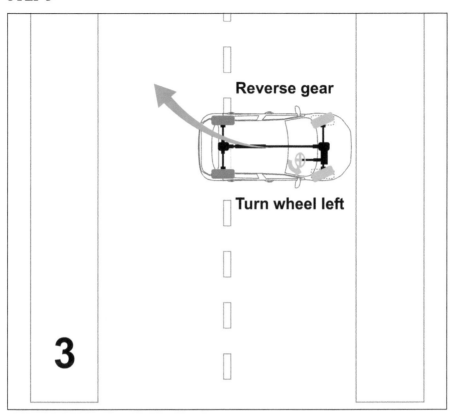

Reverse gear

Turn wheel left

3

STEP 4

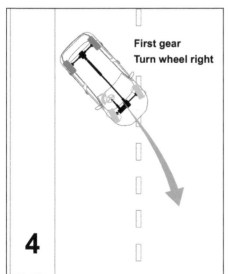

First gear
Turn wheel right

4

STEP 5

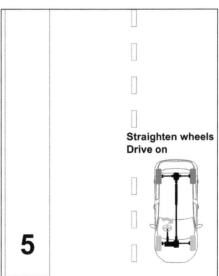

Straighten wheels
Drive on

5

✏ Practical test day advice

When you first get into the car with the driving test examiner just remember that at this point you have a 'full' licence up until the point that you say 'no thanks'.

The examiner doesn't mark all the actions that you carry out safely and correctly, but rather marks the faults that you make as either a driving fault, Serious or Dangerous.

Keep in mind that what you might consider to be a fault, the examiner may well consider it to be too trivial to even mark down. Assume that any faults you make may not be marked down as Serious or Dangerous and keep focused on continuing to drive safely and competently.

Try not to be distracted by the examiner marking your test as he/she may be just completing his paperwork, such as entering the date etc.

Drive for yourself, by dealing with the road and traffic situations as you think fit, the same as you will after you have passed your driving test when you will be driving on your own.

While you're feeling nervous, you're no longer concentrating on your driving, and while you're concentrating on your driving you won't be feeling nervous. It's a bit like sneezing. You can keep your eyes open or you can sneeze, you can't do both at the same time!

Put ALL your attention into your driving, while you're focused on the test or the examiner, you may be about to make a driving fault or serious error.

To relieve anxiety when on your driving test, use any of the following techniques:

• View it just like another driving lesson with your driving instructor and just follow the directions given.

- Imagine you are giving the examiner a lift somewhere but you're not sure of the directions, so the examiner is telling which way to go.

- If you're into computer games you could imagine that you're 'inside' a computer game and that three people are trying to catch you out and make you fail, but you're going to be so determined that no one is going to catch you out.

- Don't let anyone on the road prevent you from getting your full driving licence: they can only do that if you didn't see or react safely to them.

- In any given situation just imagine what your driving instructor would have advised you to do, or what an experienced driver who you respect would do in that same situation.

DON'T DRIVE LIKE A 'LEARNER' DRIVER!

If you drive like a learner driver, you will stay a learner driver. The examiner wants to see if you are now ready to join the ranks of qualified drivers.

Passing your driving test doesn't mean that you are the best driver ever. Neither does failing mean that you are the most diabolical driver ever. When you pass your driving test it means that you are now ready to go out and practice on your own instead of with someone supervising you.

If you fail your driving test it means that you still need more supervision and that there are one or more areas of your driving which require more attention and practice.

Remember that the examiner is looking for four main things:

You are SAFE to Yourself

You are SAFE to other road-users

You have your vehicle under your CONTROL

You are driving legally

A FEW USEFUL EXTRAS

City driving and country roads

CITY DRIVING

Keep to the left lane – it's quicker.

Because cities are so full of traffic and space is limited, everyone is trying to get to their destination quicker than the person next to them. These people will choose the right-hand lane as their means of getting past the slow traffic already using the left lanes. The problem is that there are more people in a hurry than not in a hurry, and so there are a lot of people already in the 'overtaking' or right-hand lanes.

When you approach a set of red traffic lights, for example, you will generally see more vehicles already in the right-hand lane than in the left-hand lane. However, at traffic lights, the right-hand lane is often only for turning right, or the vehicle waiting in the right-hand lane is waiting for the traffic lights to turn to green before switching on the right-hand indicator. As a result, all the drivers in the right-hand lane who want to go straight ahead will be stuck waiting until the person at the front has been able to turn right. These drivers will then frantically try to move over to the left to avoid being held up by the driver turning right and preventing them travelling straight ahead.

By keeping to the left lane in cities, you will have fewer vehicles in your lane, and you won't get held up by drivers waiting to turn right.

When I was teaching in London, I explained the above to one of my young male pupils. After my explanation he asked me *'So which lane should I use after I have passed my driving test?'* I replied *'Use the right-hand lane, because then means I will be able to get around London quicker'*.

COUNTRY ROADS

On many country roads in the UK what is very sadly lacking are white road markings and road signs to warn road users of potential hazards such as sharp bends, road narrowing, uneven road surface etc. Many accidents on these type of roads can be attributed to a lack of more sensible hazard warnings in the form of road signs and road markings.

These roads often tend to be quite narrow and single-track in places which may need you to stop and reverse, or squeeze into a narrow passing place when meeting other traffic.

When driving on country roads, it can sometimes be very difficult to know where the road is going next because of tall hedges, trees and winding roads. Very often you will see telegraph poles, wooden poles with telephone or electricity cables strung from one to the next.

By observing these into the distance, you can often predict where the road is going to bend next, and by how much. Don't rely on them completely though, as sometimes they can disappear across the fields. Just like satellite navigation systems, only use them as a guide.

You need to anticipate meeting horse riders, cyclists, pedestrians, tractors and trailers with wide loads, as well as wild animals and possible farm animals, like cows or sheep who may have escaped or are being moved from neighbouring fields. Be prepared to drive very slowly approaching bends and even slow down to walking speed, selecting low gears until you can see the way ahead is clear to increase speed again.

Although many country roads are national speed limit (60mph) areas, remember the upper speed limit is NOT a target or should be regarded as such. Just as in 20mph, 30mph, 40mph speed limit areas, it could still be inappropriate to be driving at the absolute legal maximum of these speed limits, because of the layout of the road, buildings, other road users or obstructions creating blind spots. You should only drive at a speed which you can see to be safe and clear and which, in the event of an emergency, would allow you to pull up and stop safely.

Other drivers

When other drivers make dangerous or silly decisions which put you or other road-users at risk, don't get annoyed or upset. Look upon it that these selfish drivers are just giving you even more experience of what to look out and be aware of.

Refuse to give in to the temptation to get annoyed or 'get even' with the other driver, because if you think that the other driver is driving selfishly or dangerously, guess what? So do the other drivers around you. Rise above it and set the good example by driving sensibly and courteously, as this too can be infectious.

Unfortunately, the driver you are witnessing making these poor or selfish decisions isn't alone, there are many of them out there. But you don't know exactly when they are going to turn up near you, so you will need to rely on your good judgement. Ironically, they are relying on you not to drive in the same poor and unsafe driving style as themselves.

This is why at all times you need to be constantly monitoring your mirrors, speed and awareness of what is going on around you. This is also why you cannot afford to be distracted by using mobile phones, setting the sat-nav, eating, drinking, putting on your make-up, shaving, rummaging in the glove-box, changing the music, or anything else.

What car to buy

When choosing your first car, opt for the smaller, less expensive car that is reliable and not going to keep costing you money by breaking down. Something that is 4-7 years old, perhaps. The chances are that you will put a few scratches or dents on it as you're gaining experience over the first couple of years: even if you can afford it, I wouldn't advise going for an expensive car.

If you buy your car from a car dealer you will normally have at least a 1-3 month warranty, or have the option to take out a 12-month warranty for a fee. You will also have certain statutory rights and can, if you experience problems, get repairs done by the dealer or get your money refunded. If you buy from a private seller, you buy 'as seen', so have little legal comeback if the car suffers problems after you have bought it.

Driving at night

It is never a good idea to look at the headlights coming towards you. Apart from the fact that they will blind you, you can easily miss a hazard on your nearside. Not only that, but we instinctively steer toward what we are looking at.

Some people find the bright lights of the cars coming towards them to be intimidating. A good tip when you are driving at night, particularly on an unlit road, is not to look at the headlights of the vehicle that you are driving towards, but keep watching the verge. There might be someone walking in front wearing dark clothes, there might be somebody on a bicycle with no lights on. If you're looking at the verge you will spot them that much sooner.

It is a known fact that the 'speed and distance' of approaching traffic is much more difficult to assess at night on a dark or unlit road. This is because at night all we can really see is a pair of headlights approaching. We don't have many clues to tell us what type of vehicle it is. We also have limited vision of static landmarks with which to make an assessment of the speed of the approaching vehicle.

What we may not realise, is the number of assessments we are making with the benefit of daylight. For example, in daylight we see that it is a tractor approaching, which we know will most probably not be travelling towards us as fast as a heavy goods vehicle (HGV). But on seeing an HGV, we know it probably won't be travelling as quickly as a modern car. We can also see the surroundings, such as buildings, fields, bridges etc, which are static and more accurately gauge the speed of the oncoming moving vehicle in relation to the static background.

Therefore, at night you need to be much more cautious when emerging into approaching traffic and if in any doubt whatsoever... **don't!**

What to do if you have an accident

In the event of an accident, the very first thing you need to do is make sure everybody's safe. If there are any injuries, then you need to attend to them. Importantly, you don't want anybody else to crash into you or any other vehicles involved, so if you can, get other people to direct the traffic.

If there are any serious injuries, then you need to call 999. Pretty much everybody has a mobile phone, if you don't have one, someone else will – pedestrians, locals or even a passing motorist.

If there's nobody injured and there is no further risk to anyone's safety, check for damage. I would suggest that, as nowadays as most mobile phones have cameras, take photographic evidence of any damage to both your car and the other vehicle.

Take down the registration number of the other vehicle, the make of the car, and the time of the accident too. Ask the other driver for their details: you will need their name, address, phone number and their insurance details. If nothing else, make sure you get their name, address and phone number, as insurance details can be found out later on.

It can be particularly helpful to have a note of any mobile phone numbers: if they were talking on the phone at the time of the accident, the insurance companies will be able to check their phone records to confirm that the accident was not your fault. This is another reason why it is important to make a note of the time of the accident.

> From an insurance point of view, never admit liability, even if it is your fault. This might sound a bit harsh, but it weakens your case with the insurance companies, as they will want to fight it out between themselves. They'll take care of that, you don't have to.

Finally, make a note of any other details surrounding the accident including the weather conditions, and where it happened, including the name of the road if you know.

It isn't worth getting into an argument with anyone - just exchange details and if your car is drivable, get on your way. If the car isn't driveable, get in touch with whatever car recovery service you might be signed up to.

If anyone is injured, no matter how slight, the police will also need to be informed. They should also be contacted if you think the other person could be under the influence of drugs or drink, or was just driving recklessly. Unless there are any injuries, if it's a run of the mill 50/50 accident, the police don't have to be involved.

Final Thought

The general difference between Male and Female drivers, particularly when learning to drive:

With the male driver the 'Confidence' tends to come before the 'Ability'. The male driver tends to think that they can do something which can sometimes be beyond their ability.

With the female driver the 'Ability' tends to come before the 'Confidence'. The female driver tends to be able to do something but doubts whether they are capable.

USEFUL LINKS
AND RESOURCES

Highway code:
https://www.gov.uk/guidance/the-highway-code

Buy the highway code:
https://www.safedrivingforlife.info/shop/product/official-highway-code-new-edition-2015

Download the highway code:
https://www.gov.uk/guidance/the-highway-code

Theory Practice:
https://www.gov.uk/take-practice-theory-test

Apply for your provisional licence:
https://www.gov.uk/apply-first-provisional-driving-licence

Changes to the driving test in December 2017:
https://www.gov.uk/driving-test/changes-december-2017

Changes to 'show me tell me' questions:
https://www.gov.uk/government/publications/car-show-me-tell-me-vehicle-safety-questions

Penalty points and endorsements:
https://www.gov.uk/penalty-points-endorsements/endorsement-codes-and-penalty-points

The Practical Driving Test fees:
http://www.dsa.gov.uk

Martin Caswell's websites:
http://www.LearnToDriveanEasierWay.com
http://www.DrivingTestNerves.com